RHYL TO BANGOR

Vic Mitchell and Keith Smith

MP Middleton Press

Front cover: One of the shortest named trains was "The Welsh Dragon" and it is seen leaving Colwyn Bay behind 2-6-2T no. 41287 in about 1952. Few named trains had no corridors. (R.S.Carpenter)

Back cover upper: No. 37418 East Lancashire Railway *was in EWS livery when it was recorded close to the sea near Colwyn Bay on 15th May 1999. It was hauling the 12.07 Birmingham New Street to Holyhead. (P.Jones)*

Back cover lower: An unexpected occupant of Colwyn Bay station for many years was Firefly. *It was built by Hudswell Clark as no. 1864 and was photographed on 7th July 1991. The 0-6-0T was used by the National Coal Board, formed part of a themed restaurant here and was moved to the Dartmoor Railway in 2000, to allow alterations to the station. (M.Dart/Transport Treasury)*

Published March 2012

ISBN 978 1 908174 15 4

Design Deborah Esher

Published by
Middleton Press
Easebourne Lane
Midhurst
West Sussex
GU29 9AZ
Tel: 01730 813169
Fax: 01730 812601
Email: info@middletonpress.co.uk
www.middletonpress.co.uk

Printed in the United Kingdom by Henry Ling Limited, at the Dorset Press, Dorchester, DT1 1HD

INDEX

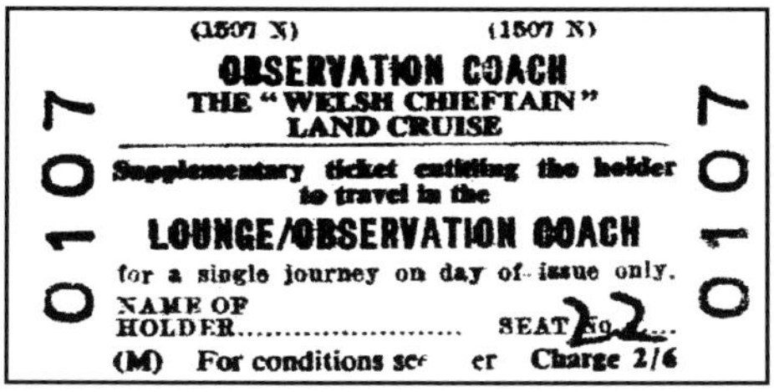

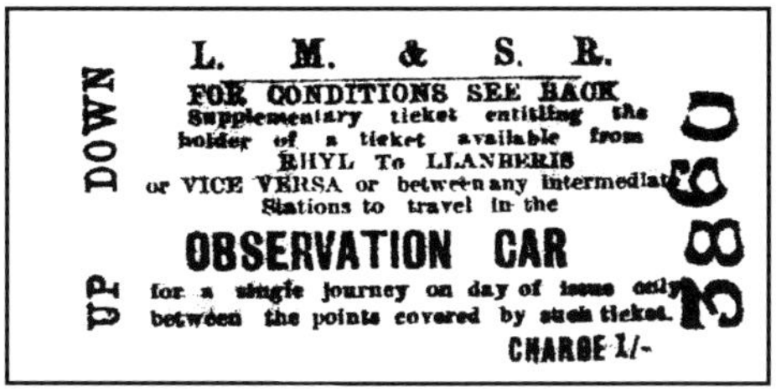

ACKNOWLEDGEMENTS

We are very grateful for the assistance received from many of those mentioned in the credits, also to B.Bennett, A.R.Carder, G.Croughton, S.C.Jenkins, F.Hornby, M.A.N.Johnston, N.Langridge, B.Lewis, Mr D. and Dr S.Salter, D.G.Smith, T.Walsh and in particular, our always supportive wives, Barbara Mitchell and Janet Smith.

I. Route map in the 1930s. (Railway Magazine)

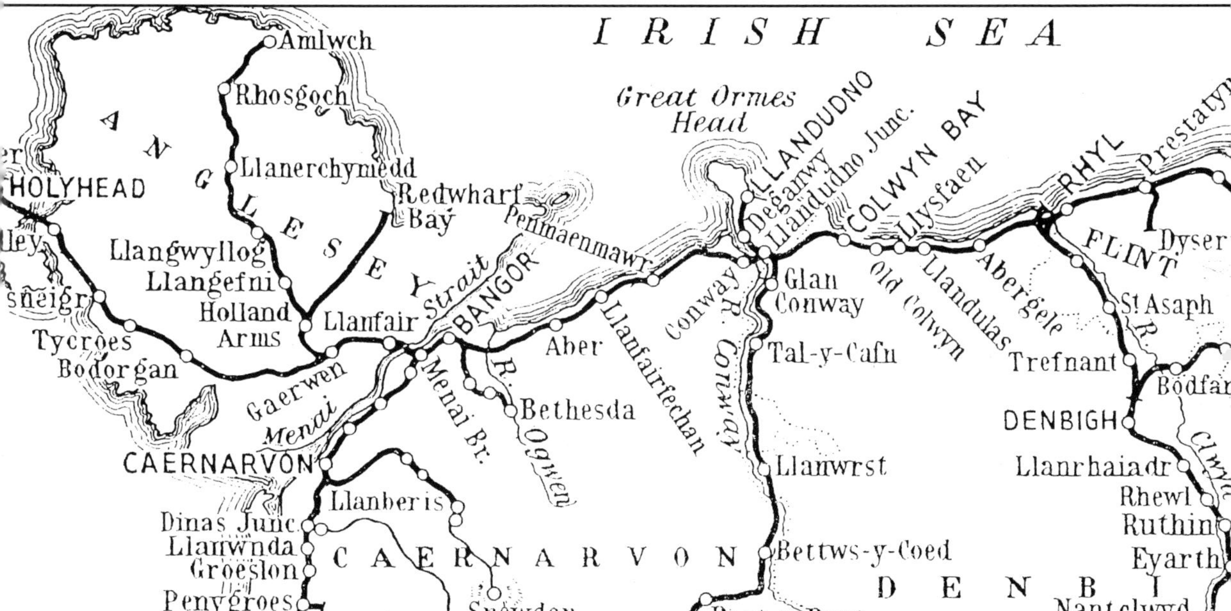

GEOGRAPHICAL SETTING

First we will look at the geology of the journey, as this has influenced tourism and the mineral wealth of the district. Beach sand near the Clwyd estuary, west of Rhyl, was extracted into the first part of the 20th century and the area was suitable for the creation of a lake in 1900 for pleasure pursuits. The coast as far as Colwyn Bay was attractive to holiday makers and was used for seabathing, even before the arrival of the railway. The environs of Rhyl became the "Blackpool of North Wales" and there was a pier from 1867, for just over 100 years.

Limestone reaches the coast on both sides of Colwyn Bay and also west of Llandudno, where it forms the impressive Great Ormes Head. The limestone outcrop between the towns is Little Ormes Head and the line climbs over its southward extension.

West of the wide estuary of the River Conway is a level area of wind blown sand and alluvium. This also forms the flat expanse between Llandudno and Deganwy.

The remainder of the journey is at the foot of massive cliffs formed by a large area of high ground, which is visited by few. Initially the line runs along the northern boundary of the Conway Mountain, which is of volcanic origin. Next comes the granite outcrops at Penmaenmawr, which have proved to be of great value for road making and thus an area of great ugliness has resulted.

The splendid views across the Irish Sea are a compensation for tourists. Many enjoy the environs of Bangor, which has had a cathedral since 975 and a university college since 1884.

The other mineral of economic importance in the area is slate. It has been worked in the Bethesda district for generations and was the reason for the construction of the branch line and also Port Penrhyn.

The line from Rhyl to the Conway was built partly in Flintshire, but mostly in Denbighshire. West of the river it was in Caernarvonshire, as it was spelt for a long period.

The Afon Clwyd is crossed on the western edge of Rhyl and the River Dulas at Llandulas. The Afon Aber is passed over west of Llanfairfechan. The Afon Ogwen and the Afon Cegin are spanned on the approach to Bangor.

The maps are to the scale of 25ins to 1 mile, with north at the top, unless otherwise indicated. Welsh spelling and hyphenation has varied over the years and so we have generally used the form of the period.

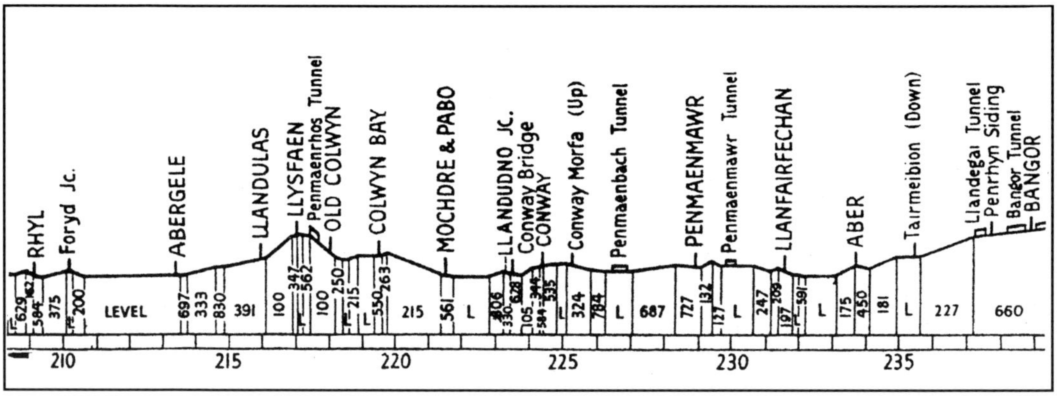

HISTORICAL BACKGROUND

The Chester & Holyhead Railway received its Act on 4th July 1844 and Robert Stephenson was appointed engineer. It was opened between Chester and Bangor on 1st May 1848 and was operated by the London & North Western Railway from the outset. This company acquired the C&HR on 18th March 1859.

The line south from Rhyl was opened by the Vale of Clwyd Railway to Denbigh in 1858 and it was in use until 1968. A short line north to Foryd Pier was open from 1859 until 1959.

Llandudno was served by the St. George's Railway & Harbour Company from 1st October 1858, this becoming part of the LNWR in 1873. South from Llandudno Junction was the line of the Conway & Llanrwst Railway, which came into use in 1863.

Bethesda's branch was opened on 1st July 1884, by the LNWR. It carried passengers until 3rd December 1951 and goods until 7th October 1963.

The LNWR became a constituent of the London Midland & Scottish Railway in 1923 and its area formed the London Midland Region of British Railways upon nationalisation in 1948.

Privatisation brought trains of Wales & West on 13th October 1996. The name was Wales & Borders from 6th November 2001 and Arriva Trains Wales from 7th December 2003. Long distance services were worked by Virgin Trains from 9th March 1997. North Western Trains operated services from Lancashire from 2nd March 1997 until 2004, when ATW took over.

PASSENGER SERVICES

The initial timetable showed four trains on weekdays, with two on Sundays. Four months after opening, this was increased to six and three. Subsequent sample Summer services between Rhyl and Llandudno Junction are listed, in the down direction. Saturday extras are excluded, but were often numerous.

	Weekdays	Sundays
1849	5	3
1859	8	4
1869	13	5
1889	15	5
1924	16	5
1939	48	12
1958	41	5
1985	25	13
2011	29	19

About half the trains terminated at Llandudno from the 1880s and many of the others were provided with a connection at Llandudno Junction (initially Conway) to Llandudno. Local trains between Llandudno and Bangor or Holyhead have been quite common since the end of steam. In some years in the 1930s, there was one train between Llandudno and Llanfairfechan, on weekdays.

Bethesda Branch

The table shows frequency in sample years.

In some years, an additional train was run on Saturdays. The final service was depleted, due to a fuel crisis.

	Weekdays	Sundays
1885	6	6
1914	12	0
1934	18	10
1947	8	0
1951	3	0

LONDON, CREWE, CHESTER, RHYL, COLWYN BAY, LLANDUDNO, BANGOR, HOLYHEAD, and DUBLIN.—L. & N. W.

Week Days.

Miles from Crewe.	Down.	aft	aft	aft	aft		mrn	mrn	mrn	mrn		mrn	mrn	mrn	mrn	mrn	mrn		mrn	mrn	mrn	mrn	mrr	mrn	aft	mrn		mrn	mrn	mrn	mrn
	324 Euston ......dep.	8 40	9 30	9L40	1145																											
	324 Birmingham (New St.) "	10 15	1015	11R0	2§55															7 15						9 10		9 10			
	390a Manchester (L. R.) .. "	10 30	1145	11r45																8 15						9 30		10 0			
	Crewe ......dep.	12 7	1 12	1 50	5 0								8 5							9 22	9 45					1055		11 0			
3¼	Worleston	mrn	mrn	mrn	mrn								8 12															1111			
8	Calveley												8 21															1120			
10½	Beeston Castle & Tarporley *												8 28							9 37								1126			
14½	Tattenhall Road												8 38															1135			
18	Waverton 368 ....[385, 386												8 47																		
21½	Chester † 72, 374, 379, arr.	12 35		2 18	5 35								8 58							9 56	1021							1155			
—	378 Manchester (Exch.) dep.	10‡20												7 30						7 50									1020		
—	378 Warrington (Bk Qy.) "	11 55										7 25		8 22						8 59				9 52					1110		
—	384 Liverpool (Lime St.) "	10X50												7 25					8 25	8 25										1050	1110
—	375 Birkenhead (W'dside) "	10K35								6 30		7 30		7 55					8 55	8 55	9 25			9 45						1055	
—	Chester (General) ......dep.	12 43	Except Monday Mornings. Sleeping Saloons, London to Holyhead.	2 36					5 55	7 30		8 35		9 10		9 15			9 50	10 5	1025			1040						12 5	
27	Sandycroft	Irish Mail.—Sleeping Saloons, London to Holyhead. Arrives Holyhead Pier at 2 35 mrn.								7 40		8 45				9 25								1050							
28¼	Queen's Ferry									7 44		8 54				9 29						Except Saturdays.	Saturdays only.	1055		Saturdays only.					
29½	Shotton 526									7 49		9 0				9 33								11 0							
30½	Connah's Quay								6 11	7 54						9 38								11 5							
33¾	Flint			2 54					6 18	8 1				9 28		9 45								1112							
35¾	Bagillt								6 25	8 9						9 52								1119							
38	Holywell Junction 384								6 30	8 15						9 58								1125							
41½	Mostyn								6 36	8 24						10 6								1133							
44½	Talacre								6 45	8 31						1012								1140							
47½	Prestatyn 378								6 52	8 38				9 50		1019								1148					1216	1240	
51½	Rhyl 386b ...... arr.			3 19					7 1	8 47				9 59		1028			1028	10 47	11 5			1157		12 7			1227	1251	1 0
	dep.			3 25					7 7	8 52				10 5					1034	10 52	1110	11 5	1115			1212			1232	1256	1 6
52½	Foryd									8 57												1110	1120								
55½	Abergele and Pensarn								7 15	9 4										11 0		1117	1127							1 4	1 14
58	Llandulas								7 23	9 12												1125	1135								
59	Llysfaen								7 27	9 16												1129	1139								
60	Old Colwyn								7 33	9 22												1134	1144								
61½	Colwyn Bay			3H42					7 37	9 26				1021					1050	11 13	1126	1138	1148			1228			1248	1 20	1 30
63¼	Mochdre and Pabo								7 46	9 35												1146	1156								
65½	Llandudno Jn. 386a .. arr.			3 54					7 53	9 41				1033					11 2	11 25	1138	1152	12 2			1240				1 32	1 41
80½	386a Bettws-y-Coed ‡ .. arr.			5 41					8 49	1044				1119						12 59	1259	1259	1259								
69	386 Llandudno ...... arr.			4 45					8 42	9 58				11 0						12V10	12 0	1210	1220			1 0		1 15			2 0
	dep.								7P40					1015					1045	10 45										1 20	
—	Llandudno Junction ...dep.			4 5					8 0					1039			1050		11 8	11 32										1 37	
66½	Conway								8 4								1053		1112	11 36	Saturdays only.				Thursdays only.					1 41	Saturdays only. Commencing on 12th instant.
71	Penmaenmawr								8 14								11 3		1123	11 47										1 52	
73¾	Llanfairfechan								8 20								11 9		1130	11 53										1 59	
75¾	Aber								8 26								1114			11 58										2 5	
81	Bangor § 385 386a ... arr.			4 28					8 37					11 1			1125		1145	12 9										2 16	
89¾	386a Carnarvon ...... arr.			5 5					9 26								12 2			1 21											
98½	386a Afonwen ...... "			6 9					1028											2 47											
—	Bangor ......dep.			4 50			7 50	8 30	9 0						1110					12 19					1245						
82½	Menai Bridge §						7 54	8 35	9 4						1114				Mondays, Fridays, and Saturdays.	12 30					1249					Mondays, Fridays, and Saturdays.	
84¼	Llanfair						8 1	8 41	9 12						1120					12 37					1257						
87½	Gaerwen 386b ...... arr.			5 5			8 7	8 47	9 18						1126					12 43					1 3						
	dep.			5 10			8 10		9 23											12 48											
93¾	Bodorgan						8 20	One class only.	9 34											12 58											
96¼	Ty Croes						8 27		9 42											1 5											
98¾	Rhosneigr						8 33		9 48											1 11											
102¼	Valley						8 40		9 58											1 20											
105¾	Holyhead 733a ...... arr.	2 25	3 22	5 55			8 50		10 7											1 29											
165¾	Kingstown Pier ‖ .. arr.	6 2																													
170½	Dublin (by Steamer) "	6F30	8N15																												

June 1920

LONDON, CREWE, CHESTER, LLANDUDNO, BANGOR, and HOLYHEAD.

Week Days.

Miles from Crewe.	Down.	aft	aft		mrn	ngt.	mrn		mrn	mrn	mrn			mrn	mrn	mrn	mrn	mrn	aft	mrn	
	412 LONDON (Euston)...dep.	8 45	11 0			12 35								2 35							
	412 Rugby ...... "	10 25	11K6			2c12								4 18							
	413 Birmingham (New St.) "	10 15	10K50			3 12											7 15				
	413 Stafford ...... "	11 2	12K30			4 10								5 24			8 29				
	522 Manchester (L.R.).. "	10 30	11K45											6 0			8 35				
	626 Stoke-on-Trent...... "	11 5												6 55			8 30				
	Crewe ......dep.	12 8	2 0			5 0								8 12			9 25				
3¼	Worleston	mrn	mrn											8 18							
8½	Calveley	Irish Mail.												8 25							
10¾	Beeston Castle & Tarporley I													8 31			9 40				
14½	Tattenhall Road													8 39							
18	Waverton 518..[513,517,519													8 45							
21½	Chester A 111, 506, arr.	12 35	2 27			5 33								8 53			9 56				
36½	506 Birkenhead F ...... arr.		4 10			7 15								9 32			10 32				
—	437 Preston ......dep.	10 50									5 35						7 34				
—	516 Manchester (Exch.) "	10T20									5 50			7 25			8 40				
—	516 Warrington (B.Q.).. "	11 55									7 25			8 9			9 20				
—	518 Liverpool (Lime St.) "	10X45	11a50								6 0			7 25			8 25				
—	508 Birkenhead F ..... "	11P20							6 0	6 30	7 35			8 15		8 15	9 18			9 35	
—	Chester (General) ......dep.	12 43	2 47			5 52	6 28		6 45	7 30	8 30		Through Carriages Manchester (Ex.) to Bangor.	9 2		9 10	10 0			1030	
27	Sandycroft	1st & 3rd class Sleeping accommodation and Thro' Carriages, London to Holyhead.					6 37		6 55	7 39	8 39					9 19				1039	
28¾	Queen's Ferry					6 3	6 41		6 59	7 43	8 43					9 23				1043	
29½	Shotton					6 7	6 44		7 4	7 47	8 46					9 26				1046	
30½	Connah's Quay					6 13	6 47		7 7	7 52	8 50					9 30				1050	
33¾	Flint					6 21	6 58		7 15	7 59	8 57			9 18	On 3rd Wednesday in month.	9 37				1057	
35¾	Bagillt						7 5		Stop	8 5	9 2					9 42				11 2	
38	Holywell Junction (below) ...					6 31	7 15			8 11	9 8					9 50				11 8	
41¾	Mostyn					6 40	7 24			8 19						9 58				1116	
44½	Talacre						7 30			8 25						10 4				1122	
47¾	Prestatyn					6 51	7 40		mrn	8 31				9 36		1010	10 36			1128	
51½	Rhyl 496		3 22			7 2	7 48		7 55	8 39				9 44	10 0	1018	10 44			1136	
55½	Abergele and Pensarn					7 12			8 4	8 48					10 7		10 54			1149	
58½	Llandulas					7 20			8 11	8 55										1156	
60¾	Old Colwyn					7 27			8 17	9 1				9 59						12 2	
61¾	Colwyn Bay		3H43			7 33			8 21	9 5				10 3			11 5			12 6	
65¾	Llandudno Jn. 504 ...... arr.		3 56			7 45			8 30	9 14				1013			11 16			1215	
69	493 Llandudno ...... arr.		4 44			8 14			8 45	9 40				1030			11 35			1230	
80½	504 Bettws-y-Coed B.... "		5 31			8 32								1110						1254	
—	Llandudno Junction .....dep.		4 6			8 0			8 33	9 20				1019			11 20	1130		1230	
66¾	Conway					8 3				9 23							11 23	1133		1233	
71	Penmaenmawr					8 12				9 31				1028				1142		1242	
73¾	Llanfairfechan					8 20				9 37				1035				1149		1249	
75¾	Aber					8 26				9 42								1154		1255	
81	Bangor C 499, 514 ...... arr.		4 26			8 36			8 54	9 51				1046			11 43	12 3		1 4	
89¾	514 Caernarvon ...... arr.		5 4			9 22			9 22					1111			12 11			1 29	
108¾	514 Afon Wen ...... "		6 4			10 24			1024								1 6				
112¾	140 Pwllheli ...... "		6 35			10 36			1036								1 35				
111¼	141 Criccieth ...... "		6 25			10 56			1056								1 26				
116¾	141 Portmadoc ...... "		6 35			11 9			11 9								1 35				
—	Bangor ......dep.		4 50		7 45				9 5					11 0			12 0		1235		
82¾	Menai Bridge C				7 49				9 9					11 4			12 4		1239		
84½	Llanfair				7 54				9 14					1110			12 9		1244		
87½	Gaerwen 505 ...... arr.		5 1		8 0				9 20					1116			12 15		1250		
	dep.		5 6		8 3				9 23								12 18				
93¾	Bodorgan				8 12				9 32								12 27				
96¼	Ty Croes				8 20				9 40								12 35				
98¾	Rhosneigr				8 25				9 45								12 40				
102¼	Valley				8 33				9 53								12 48				
105¾	Holyhead ...... arr.	2 25	5 43		8 40				10 0								12 55				
165¾	Kingstown Pier D.. "	5 50																			
170¾	Dublin G 1103...... "	6 35																			

April 1932

Table 99 LONDON, CREWE, CHESTER, LLANDUDNO, BANGOR, and HOLYHEAD

Week Days

Miles from Crewe		p.m	p.m	am	a.m	a.m	a.m	a.m	a.m	a.m	am	a m	a.m	a.m	a.m	a.m	p.m	p.m	a.m	a.m	p.m	a.m	a.m	p.m	a.m	p.m	a.m	a.m	p.m	p.m
		IRISH MAIL; SC and RC London (Euston) to Holyhead (see note Z); Steamer dep. Holyhead 3 25 a.m. Arr. Dublin (W. Row) 7 23 a.m	RC Crewe to Holyhead		RC Bangor to Amlwch (Table 102)	RC Bangor to Pwllheli	RC Bangor to Amlwch (Table 102)		RC Chester to Bangor			RC Chester to Llandudno		RC L'pool (L.St.) to Bangor	Saturdays only; RC Bangor to Amlwch (Table 102)	RC Crewe to Llandudno and Holyhead	RC Bangor to Pwllheli	To Amlwch (Table 102)	Except Saturdays; Except Sats.	Saturdays only	Saturdays only	Saturdays only; RC Crewe to Llandudno	Except Saturdays	Saturdays only		RC Bangor to Pwllheli	RC M'chester (Ex.) to Llandudno & Holyhead	To Amlwch (Table 102)	Saturdays only RC Liverpool (L. St.) to Rhyl; RC Bangor to Afonwen	Except Saturdays
	50 LONDON (Euston) .... dep	8H45	10Z45	..	..	..	..	..	..	..	..	12F2	..	..	..	..	..	..	..	..	..	..	7R55	..	8R30	..		10 R 0		..
	50 BIRMINGHAM (N. St.). "	10H10	11H10	..	..	..	..	..	..	..	..	3 21	..	..	..	7 10	..	..	..	..	..	9 15	9 20	..	9 50	..		11 25		..
	118 MANCHESTER (L. Rd.) "	10H25	12 35	..	..	..	..	..	..	..	..	5 50	..	-	..	8 0	..	..	..	..	..	9 15	9 15	..	..	..		11 55		..
	128 STOKE-ON-TRENT ..... "	11H5	..	..	..	..	..	..	..	..	..	6 46	..	..	..	8 10	..	..	..	..	..	1024	1024	..	..	..		12j24		..
—	Crewe .... dep	12 14	2Y 5	..	..	..	..	..	..	..	..	7 35	..	7 50	..	9 20	..	..	..	..	..	11 0	11 0	..	11u55	..		1 15		
[illegible]	Calveley		a.m	..	..	..	..	..	..	..	..	..	..	8 4	..	..	..	..	..	..	..	1113	1116	..	..	..		1 27		
[illegible]	Beeston Castle & Tarpor'y A		..	..	..	..	..	..	..	..	..	7 53	..	8 11	..	9 36	..	..	..	..	..	1120	1130	..	..	..		1 34		
14½	Tattenhall Road		..	..	..	..	..	..	..	..	..	..	..	8 18	..	..	..	..	..	..	..	-	1137	..	..	..		1 41		
18	Waverton		..	..	..	..	..	..	..	..	..	..	..	8 24	..	..	..	..	..	..	..	..	1143	..	..	..		1 48		
21¾	Chester (General) .... arr	12 40	2Y31	..	..	..	..	..	..	..	..	8 8	..	8 32	..	9 57	..	..			..	1141	1154		12 24	..		1 57		
36½	113 BIRKENHEAD (W'side) arr	..	7 5	..	..	..	..	..	..	..	..	8 48	..	9 4	..	10 38	..	..			..	1245	1245		1 19	..		2 52		
—	146 LEEDS CITY .... dep	..	10q42	..	..	..	..	..	..	..	..	Stop	3Y25	Stop	..	6 2	..	..			..	8 15			8 15	..	10 20	Stop		
—	98 MANCHESTER (Ex.) ... "	..	..	..	..	..	..	..	..	..	..		6 5		..	8 35	..	..			..	1025			10 25	..	11 55			
—	98 WARRINGTON (B. Q.) .. "	12 0	..	..	..	..	..	..	..	..	..	..	7 28	a.m	..	9 15	..	..			..	11 8			11 8	..	12 36	..		
—	117 LIVERPOOL (Lime St) "	10D45	12P10	..	..	..	..	..	..	..	..	a.m	6 32	7d50	..	..	..	..			..	..			10 45	..	..	..	1245	..
—	113 LIVERPOOL (Cen.L.L.)¶ "	10L55	..	..	..	..	..	..	..	..	..	6 15	7 25	8 15	..	9 5	..	..			..	1025			11 35	..	12u15	..	1 10	1255
—	113 BIRKENHEAD (W'side) "	11L10	..	..	..	..	..	..	..	..	550	6 30	7 35	7 50	..	9 20	..	..			..	1035			11 45	..	12u25	..	1 20	1 10
—	Chester (General) .... dep	12 52	2Y52	..		..	..	..	5 45	6 30	645	7 8	8 20	9 5		10 5	..	..	1055	1115	..	1152		..	12 35	1245	1 25	..	2 10	2 25
27	Sandycroft			..		..	..	..	5 55	..	..	7 17	8 29	..		..	..	..	11 3	1123	..			12 4	..	1253	..	..	2 18	2 34
28½	Queen's Ferry			..		..	..	..	5 59	..	657	7 21	8 33	-		..	..	..	11 7	1127	..		..	12 7	..	1257	..	..	2 22	2 38
29½	Shotton Low Level			..		..	..	..	6 4	..	..	7 24	8 35	..		..	..	..	11 9	1129	..		..	12 9	..	1259	..	..	2 24	2 40
30½	Connah's Quay			..		..	..	..	6 10	6 44	7 3	7 28	8 41	..		..	..	..	1113	1134	..		..	12 13	..	1 3	..	..	2 28	2 44
33¼	Flint			..		..	..	..	6 18	6 53	711	7 36	8 48	9 22		..	..	..	1121	1142	..		..	12 21	..	1 10	..	..	2 36	2 51
35¾	Bagillt			..		..	..	..	..	6 59	..	7 41	8 53	..		..	..	..	1127	1147	..		..	12 26	..	1 15	..	..	2 41	2 56
38	Holywell Junction			..		..	..	..	6 29	7 8	720	7 48	9 0	9 31		..	..	..	1134	1153	..		..	12o39	..	1 21	1 49	..	2 47	3 5
41½	Mostyn			..		..	..	..	6 35	7 14	Stp	7 55	9 6	..		..	..	..	1140	1159	..		..	12 45	..	1 27	..	..	2 53	3 11
44½	Talacre			..		..	..	..	..	7 20	..	8 1	9 12	..		..	..	..	1146	12 5	..		..	12 51	..	1 33	..	..	2 59	3 17
47¾	Prestatyn		..	..		..	..	..	6 49	7 27	..	8 8	9 18	9 45		10 37	..	..	1152	1211	..	1225	..	12 57	1 7	1 39	2 6	..	3 5	3 23
51½	Rhyl		3Yc32	..		..	..	..	7t10	7y55	..	8 18	9 26	9 56		10 47	..	..	12 0	1219	..	1235	..	1 4	1§18	1 46	2*19	..	3 11	3 31
55½	Abergele and Pensarn		..	..		..	..	..	7 22	8 3	..	8 26		10 4		10 55	..	..		1226	..	1243	..	..	1 27		2 27	..		..
61½	Colwyn Bay		3Y51	..		..	..	..	7 35	8 16	..	8 38	Stop	1017		11 7	..	..	Stop	1239		1255	..	..	1 41	Stop	2 42	..	Stop	..
65½	Llandudno Junction .... arr		4Y0	..		..	..	..	7 43	8 24	..	8 46	..	1025		11 15		..	..	1247		1 3	..	..	1 49	..	2 50	..	..	..
68½	105 Llandudno .... arr		4 54	..	..			..	8 1	8 45	..	9 2	..	1040		11 36		..	..	..		1 15	..	..	2 20	..	3 5	..	..	..
80½	104 BETWS-Y-COED .... "		5 33	..	..			..	8 41	..	..		a.m	1115		1 6		..	..	..		..	..	..	2‡50	..	3 42	..	..	..
—	Llandudno Junction ... dep		4Y 9	..	..			..	8 5	8 29	..		9 0	1033		11 21		..	..	1 9			..	..	1 55	..	3 2	..	..	..
66½	Conway		..	..	..			..	8 9	..	..		9 3	1036		11 25		..	..	1 14			..	..	1 59	..	3 6	..	..	..
71	Penmaenmawr		..	..	..			..	8 17	..	..		9 11	1044		11 33		..	..	1 22			..	..	2 8	..	3 14	..	..	..
73¾	Llanfairfechan		..	..	..			..	8 24	..	..		9 17	1050		11 40		..	..	1 28			..	..	2 15	..	3 21	..	..	..
75¾	Aber		..	..	..			..	8 30	..	am		9 23	1056		..		..	..	1 33			..	..	2 21	..	..	..	..	..
81	Bangor D .... arr		4g29	..	..			..	8 40	8 50	..		9 33	11 5	..	11 52	..	..	p.m	1 42	..		..	..	2 30	p.m	3 34	p.m	p.m	..
	dep		4Y41	435	5 25	5 30	6 45	7 42	..	9 12	9 0		..	1130	1140	12 3	1220	1240	1 35	..	1 50		..	..	..	2 52	3 42	3 55	4 4	..
82¼	Menai Bridge D		..	..	..	5 34	6 49	7 46	..	9 20	9 4		..	1134	1144	12 7	1224	1244	1 39	..	1 54		..	..	..	2 56	3 46	3 59	4 8	..
89½	108 CAERNARVON .... arr		..	448	..	5 49	..	..	..	..	921		..	1151	..	..	1239	..		..	..	..	..	..	..	3 13	..	..	4 23	..
108½	108 AFONWEN .... "		..	539	..	6 55	..	..	..		1020		..	1245	..	..	1 35	..		..	..	..	..	..	..	4 9	..	..	5 22	..
113	108 PWLLHELI .... "		..	635	..	7 21	..	..	..		1053		..	1 7	..	..	2 0	..		..	..	..	..	..	..	4 30	..	..	6 5	..
116½	108 PORTMADOC .... "		..	6 0	..	8 12	..	..	..		1059		..	1 16	..	..	2 4	..		..	..	..	..	..	..	4 29	..	..	5 55	..
84½	Llanfair		..	..	..	..	..	7 51	..	9 24	..	..	..		..	12 13	..	1249	1 45	..	2 0	..	..	..	..		3 52	4 5		..
87½	Gaerwen		..	..	5 37	..	7 0	8 0	..	9 33	..	..	..		1154	12 21	..	1256	1 54	..	2 9	..	..	..	..		3 59	4 11		..
93¾	Bodorgan		..	..	..	..	..	8 9	..	9 42	..	..	..		..	12 30	..		2 7	..	2 22	..	..	..	..		4 8			..
96½	Ty Croes		..	..	..	..	..	8 16	..	9 48	..	..	..		..	12 36	..		2 16	..	2 31	..	..	..	..		4 14			..
98¼	Rhosneigr		..	..	..	..	..	8 21	..	9 54	..	..	..		..	12 41	..		2 24	..	2 39	..	..	..	..		4 19			..
102¼	Valley		..	..	..	..	..	8 29	..	10 2	..	..	..		..	12 49	..		2 34	..	2 49	..	..	..	..		4 27			..
105¾	Holyhead .... arr	2 35	5‡23	..	..	..	..	8 36	..	10 9	..	..	..		..	12 58	..		2 43	..	2 58	..	..	..	..		4 34			..
165¾	Kingstown Pier F ... "	6 40	..	..	..	..	..	..	..	..	..	..	..		..	..	..		..	..	..	..	..	..	..		..			..

January 1955

BANGOR and BETHESDA (One class only).—L. M. & S.

Miles	Down.	mrn	mrn		mrn	mrn		aft	aft		aft	aft		aft		aft W	aft S					
	Bangor .... dep.	7 37	8 55	....	9 55	11 0	....	1 10	3 5	....	4 25	5 37	....	7 10	....	9 5	10 0	....	....	....	....	....
2¾	Felin Hen	7 44	9 2	....	10 2	11 7	....	1 17	3 12	....	4 32	5 45	....	7 19	....	9 14	10 9	....	....	....	....	....
3¾	Tregarth	7 50	9 8	....	10 8	1113	....	1 23	3 18	....	4 38	5 51	....	7 25	....	9 20	1015	....	....	....	....	....
5	Bethesda .... arr.	7 55	9 13	....	1013	1118	....	1 28	3 23	....	4 43	5 55	....	7 30	....	9 25	1020	....	....	....	....	....

S Saturdays only W Wednesdays and Saturdays.

July 1924

BANGOR and BETHESDA (Third class only)

Miles	Week Days only	a.m		a.m		p.m		p.m S				
	Bangor .... dep	7 25	..	8 24	..	5 35	..	9 8	..	..	..	..
2¼	Felin Hen Halt	7 32	..	8 31	..	5 42	..	9 15	..	..	..	..
3¼	Tregarth	7 36	..	8 35	..	5 46	..	9 19	..	..	..	..
4¼	Bethesda .... arr	7 40	..	8 39	..	5 50	..	9 23	..	..	..	..

Miles	Week Days only	a.m		a.m		p.m		p.m S				
—	Bethesda .... dep	7 45	..	8 42	..	5 55	..	9 25	..	..	..	..
1¼	Tregarth	7 48	..	8 45	..	5 58	..	9 28	..	..	..	..
2¼	Felin Hen Halt	7 52	..	8 49	..	6 2	..	9 32	..	..	..	..
4¼	Bangor .... arr	8 1	..	8 58	..	6 11	..	9 41	..	..	..	..

S Saturdays only

March 1951

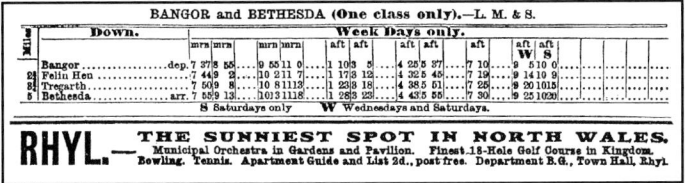

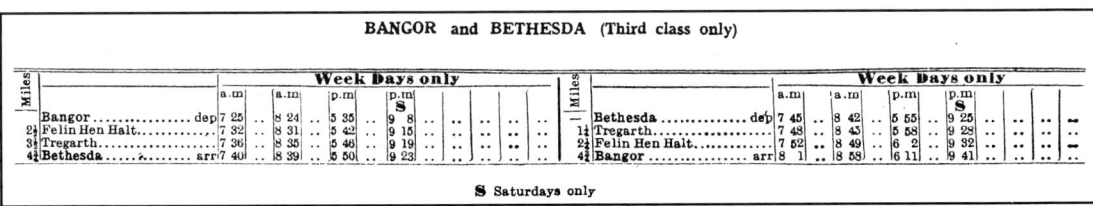

RHYL

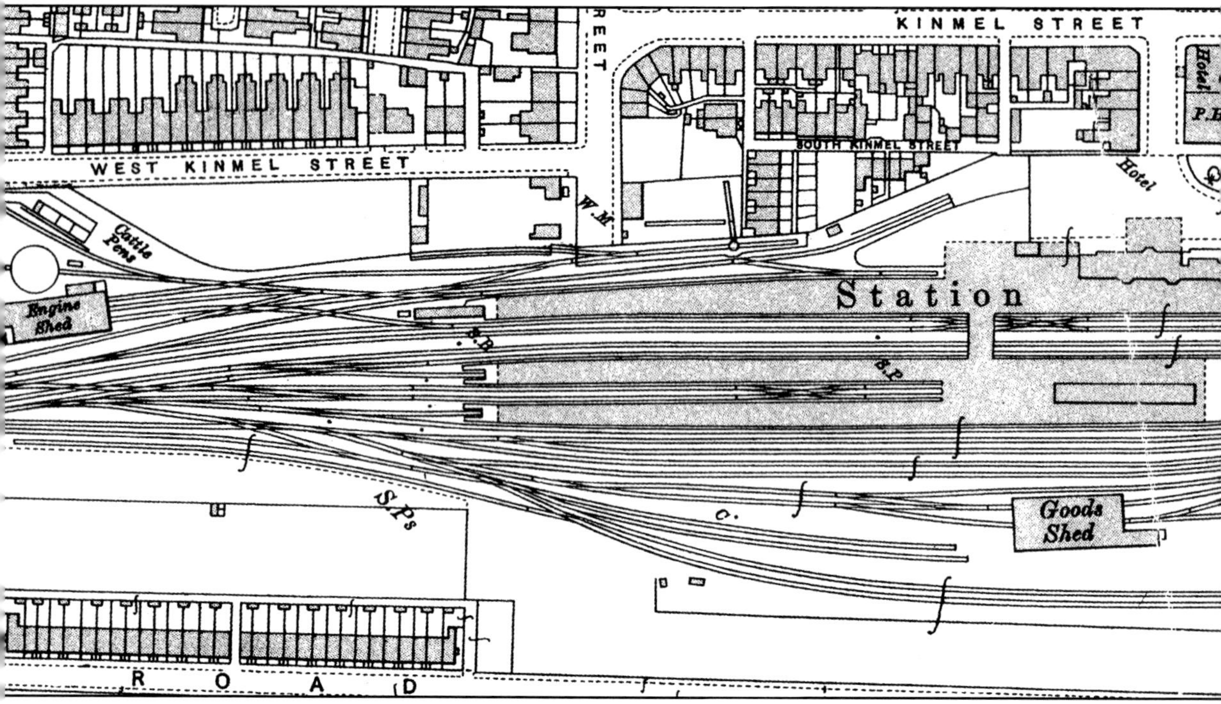

1. No. 1949 *King Arthur* is partially obscuring the sign inviting passengers to change for the Vale of Clwyd, probably in the 1920s. There is a short bay platform beyond the locomotive. (P.Q.Treloar coll.)

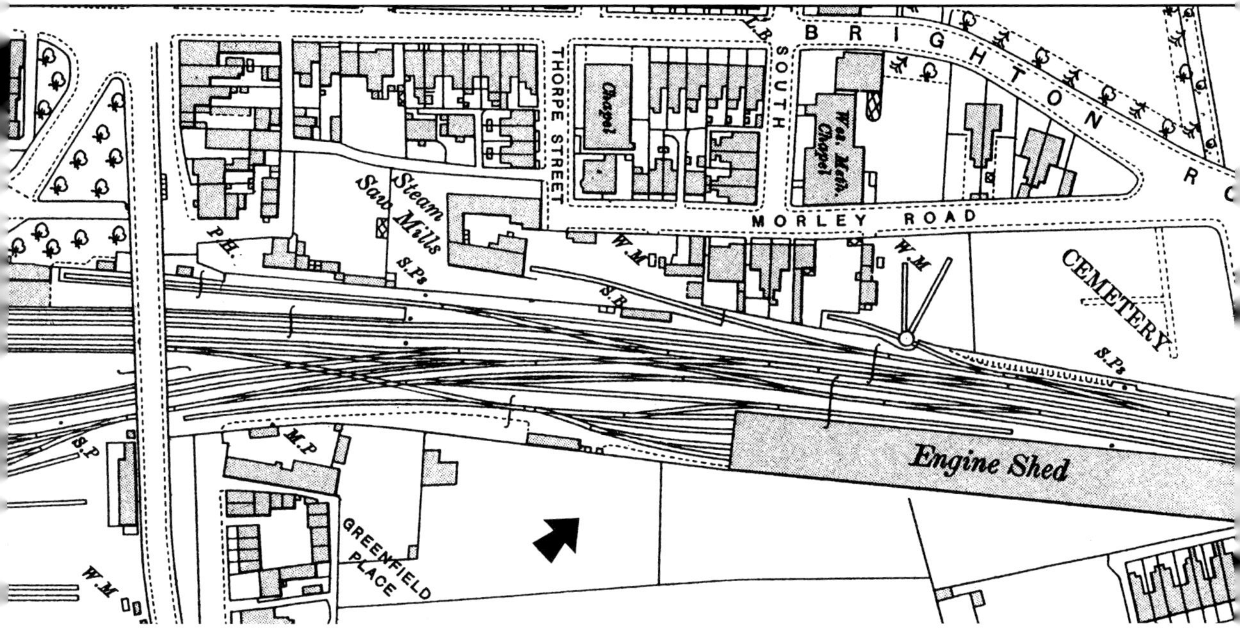

II. The engine shed shown on the right was actually a carriage shed, the real one being on the extreme left of this 1912 extract. The nearby cattle pens were removed in 1938; they had originally been east of the goods shed. A level crossing predated the bridge shown on the left of the right page, which carries Vale Road and was completed in 1878.

2. An improved station came into use in October 1901 and its north elevation was recorded in 1952. The impressive porte-cochère was demolished later. (British Railways)

3. A view west from the up platform features the through lines and the island platform. The goods office is the low building on the left. This and the shed were built in 1898. (P.Jones coll.)

4. The shed code was 7D from 1948 to 1952 and 6K until closure in 1963. No. 40589 is resting on 27th August 1954. There were 27 locomotives working from here in 1950. The first turntable came into use in mid-1849 and was intended to improve goods train operation. (H.C.Casserley)

Other views of this station can be seen in pictures 86-98 in our *Chester to Rhyl* album.

5. Standing in the shed yard on 24th August 1961 is ex-Lancashire & Yorkshire Railway 0-6-0 no. 52119. The turntable had originally been in the background. (E.Wilmshurst)

6. A view from the goods yard on 31st July 1966 shows the engine shed storing empty wagons. The water tank is to the left of it and the lamp to the left of that was still lit by gas. (R.S.Carpenter)

↓ 8. The station originally had three level crossings, but all were replaced by bridges before the end of the 19th century. This is west of the station and is seen on 9th June 1973 as no. D387 passes under with empty stock from Llandudno. It was known as H bridge, owing to its plan. (T.Heavyside)

↑ 7. It is 2nd September 1968 and a class 25 heads west near the site of the tracks to the two bay platforms for the Vale of Clwyd trains. Passenger services on that route had lasted until 1955. Its junction with the main line is shown on map VI. The 54-lever signal box there was in use until 31st May 1970. (Bentley coll.)

↓ 9. The 11.50 Manchester Victoria to Bangor DMU is regaining the main line on 6th August 1983. On the left is No. 2 Box, which was completed in 1900 and it had a 126-lever frame when closed on 26th March 1990. It was listed Grade II and was still standing 20 years later. No. 1 was still in use in 2012. (D.H.Mitchell)

WEST OF RHYL

Rhyl Miniature Railway

10. The 15ins gauge line is one of the oldest in the world and was begun in 1911. Apart from World Wars, it has operated during most Summers and five bogie coaches from pre-1920 are in regular use. Seen on 15th August 1996 is *Joan*, a 4-4-2 built by Barnes in 1920. Three others followed its success. Central Station opened in 1997 and greatly enhanced the line, which is operated by the Rhyl Steam Preservation Trust. The trains circumnavigate the attractive Marine Lake. (T.Heavyside)

III. The layout in 2005 comprised a long circuit, with three roads in Central Station, as shown. The single track is in the workshop. (RMR)

Rhyl Miniature Tramway

11. The Lancaster Electrical Company of Barnet produced a 15ins gauge tram in 1949 and operated it there. Another followed and a permanent site was sought. Thus a track was laid here and was operated from 1952 to 1957. A longer route was sought and this was found near Eastbourne. It was in use in 1955-69, using 2ft gauge. This was increased to 2ft 9ins, when the fleet was moved to Seaton and operation began there on a short length in 1971. (TLRS)

IV. Track diagram of 1952, with later alterations. (D.Voice)

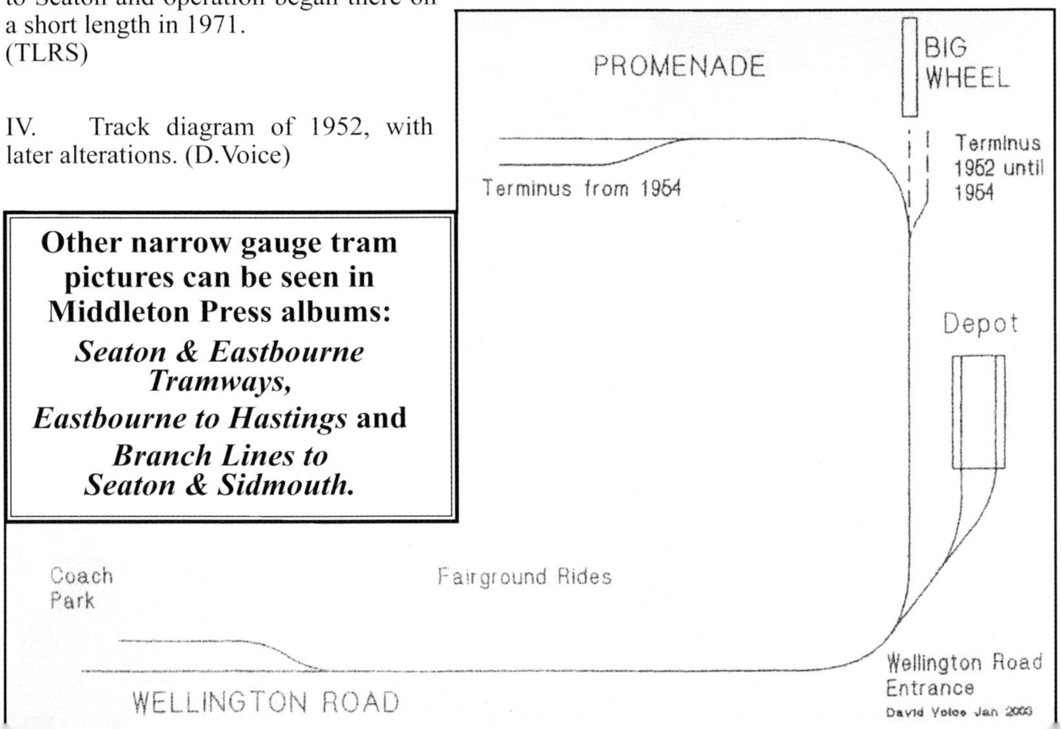

Other narrow gauge tram pictures can be seen in Middleton Press albums:
Seaton & Eastbourne Tramways,
***Eastbourne to Hastings* and**
Branch Lines to Seaton & Sidmouth.

FORYD

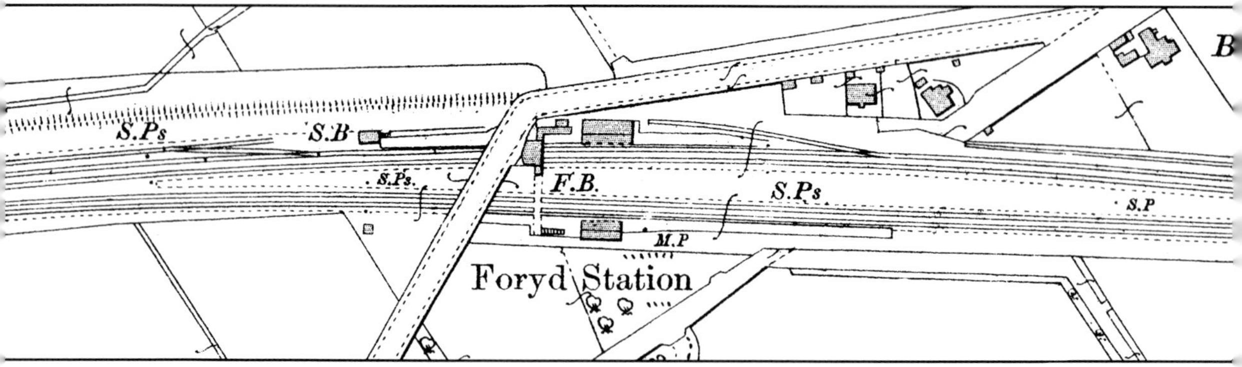

V. The first station for Foryd was on the Vale of Clwyd line and it opened on 11th May 1858. It was replaced by this one on the main line on 20th April 1885. It is seen on the 1913 edition, after quadrupling, together with the original straight alignment of the main road. This had a level crossing, which was replaced by the bridge to the left of the station. This came into use with the station, but the sharp bend at its north end presented problems to some motorists later. The siding on the left was used by the civil engineers, who had to frequently repair the sea defences. The short siding near the up platform was used for goods.

12. The booking office was on the bridge from the outset, but the down platform had to be replaced by one further south, due to the quadrupling of the tracks. The station was closed from 2nd July 1917 until 1st July 1919. It closed again on 5th January 1931, but was used briefly in the Summers of 1938 and 1939 under the name of KINMEL BAY HALT, for holiday traffic. There were seven trains calling each way on weekdays in 1924. (A.Dudman coll.)

This advertisement was on the front of Bradshaw's timetable in 1937.

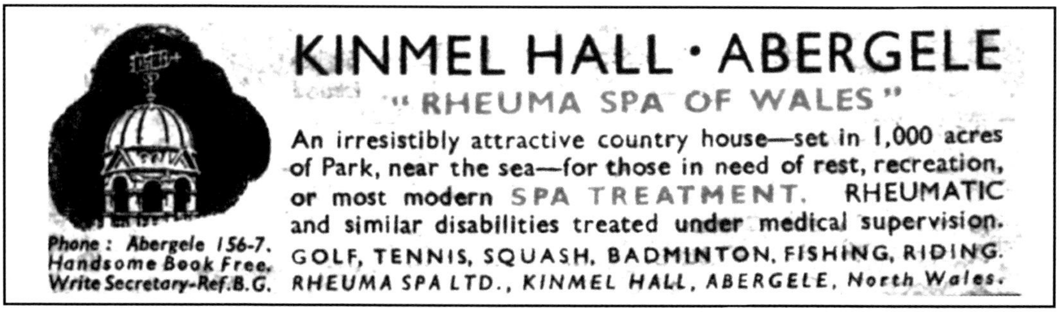

KINMEL HALL · ABERGELE
"RHEUMA SPA OF WALES"
An irresistibly attractive country house—set in 1,000 acres of Park, near the sea—for those in need of rest, recreation, or most modern SPA TREATMENT. RHEUMATIC and similar disabilities treated under medical supervision.
GOLF, TENNIS, SQUASH, BADMINTON, FISHING, RIDING.
RHEUMA SPA LTD., KINMEL HALL, ABERGELE, North Wales.
Phone: Abergele 156-7.
Handsome Book Free.
Write Secretary-Ref.B.G.

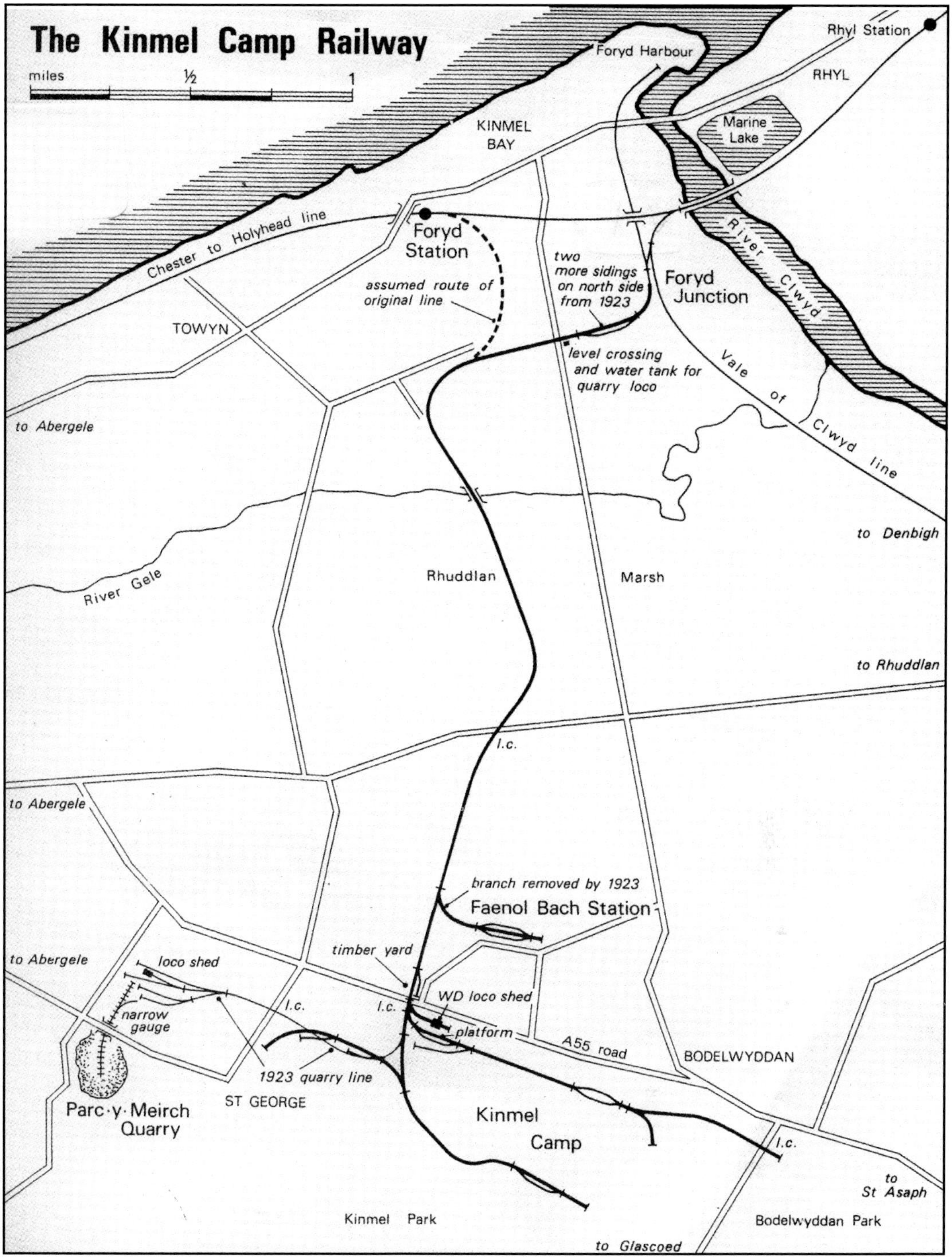

VI. Kinmel Park was used for a military camp during World War I and the line to it was completed in February 1915, an engine shed being provided at Foryd initially. The building of the camp was finished in November 1916 and two 0-6-2Ts arrived from the Woolmer Instructional Military Railway (see our *Branch Lines to Longmoor*). Direct operation to and from Rhyl was possible from April 1917 and the line opened for military personnel on 14th June 1917. Six weekday trips were operated, with three on Sundays. The four-mile journey took 35 minutes and many more locomotives arrived, there being eight at one period. Around 20,000 men were often resident here, but most of the huts were sold in 1920-22. Lime Firms Ltd took over most of the route in 1923 and an extension was completed in June. There had been a drawbridge over the River Clwyd, which was usable until 1862. (Industrial Railway Record no. 102)

13. Foryd Harbour is at the top of the map and its pier had a rail link for freight until 1959. There was a regular steamship to Liverpool for many years and this 1956 view has evidence of the weekday freight service. (G.H.Platt)

14. The limestone plant and engine shed at St. George are seen shortly after rail traffic ceased in February 1965. The graded material was destined for steelworks along the coast and in Cheshire and was moved on the branch by two 0-6-0STs in succession and finally a Hudswell Clarke diesel. (P.G.Hindley)

ABERGELE & PENSARN

15. The original building was similar to the one still to be seen at Flint. Demolition was necessary for the track quadrupling, although part survived on the down side. A new goods shed was built, slightly further south. (Lens of Sutton coll.)

16. The new station opened in July 1902 and is seen in about 1935, looking east. An island platform was never built. (Stations UK)

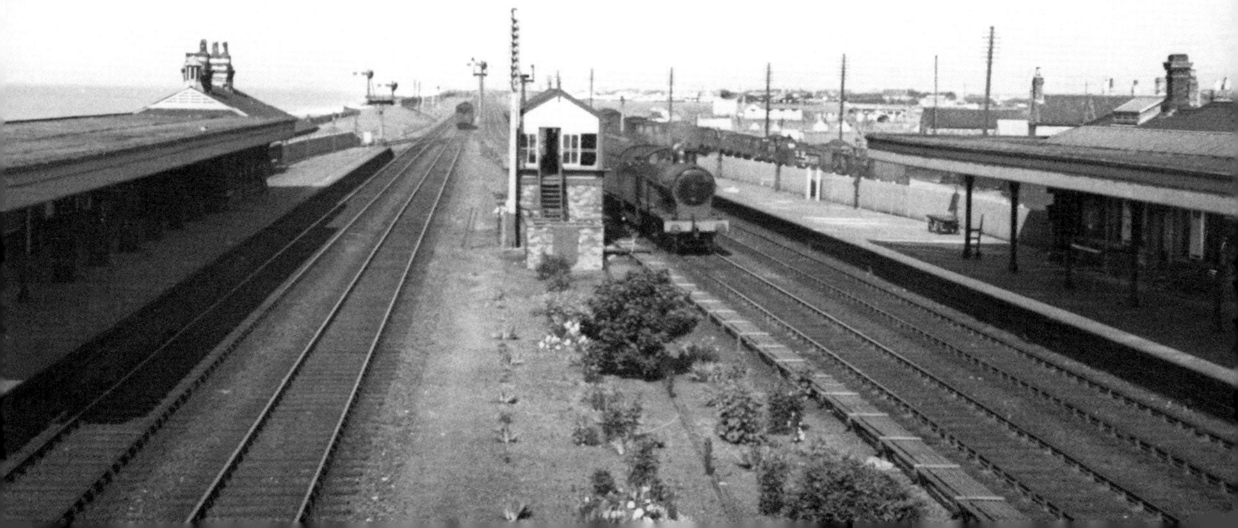

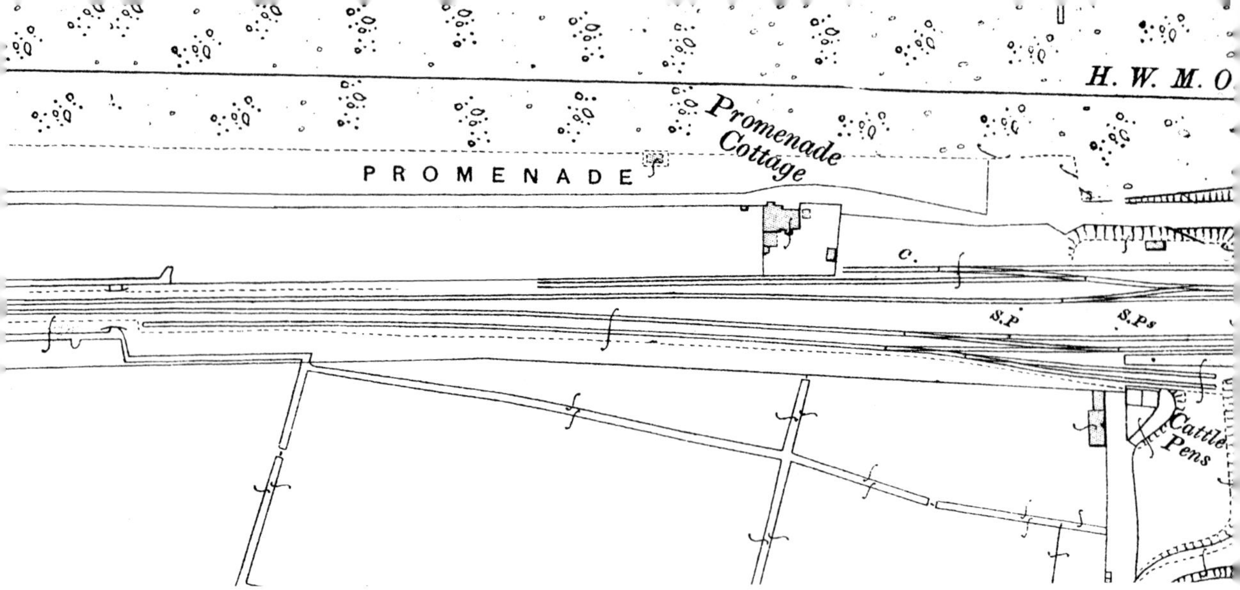

VII. The 1913 survey has the road bridge at the page join. The long fenced area to the left of the cattle pens was termed the timber yard and was provided with a 5-ton crane in later years.

Issued by the L. & N. W. R. Co., subject to the Company's regulations, and to the conditions in their Time Tables.

Abergele & Pensarn To

Rhyl

C

Third 401 RHYL Class

5116

17. This westward panorama is from the road bridge in August 1945 and includes the cattle pens. Goods traffic ceased on 1st March 1965. The double acting signal arms were needed because the bridges caused obstructions to vision. (Bentley coll.)

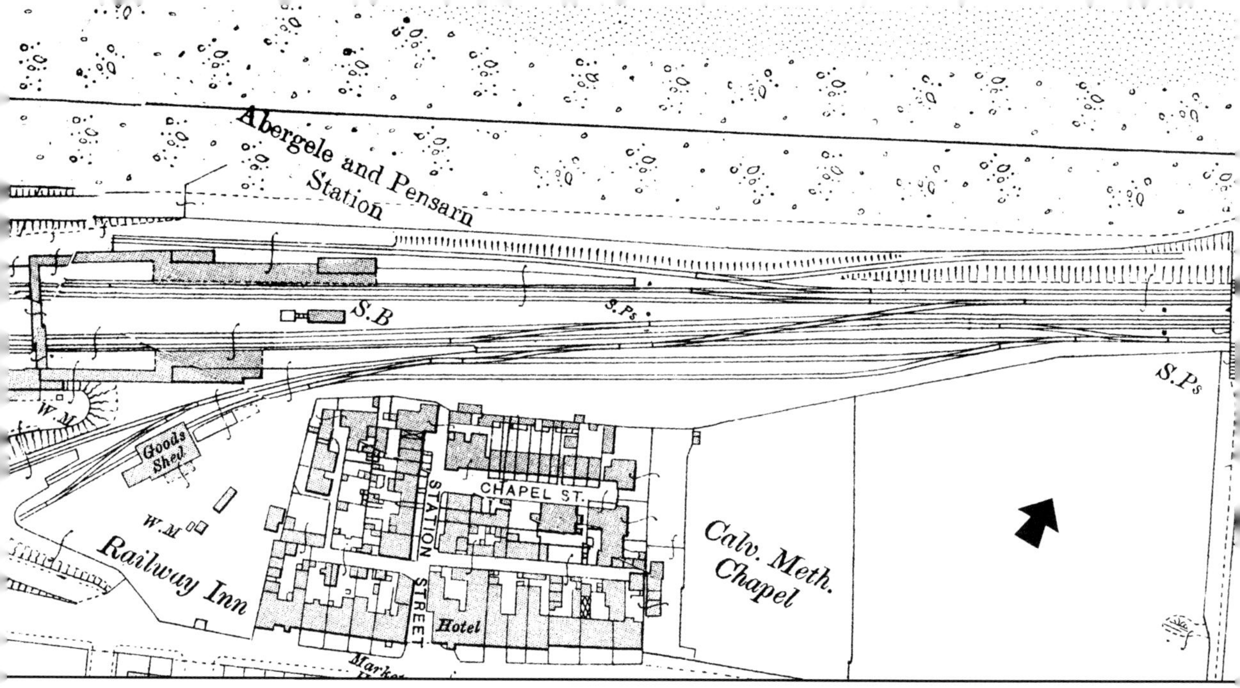

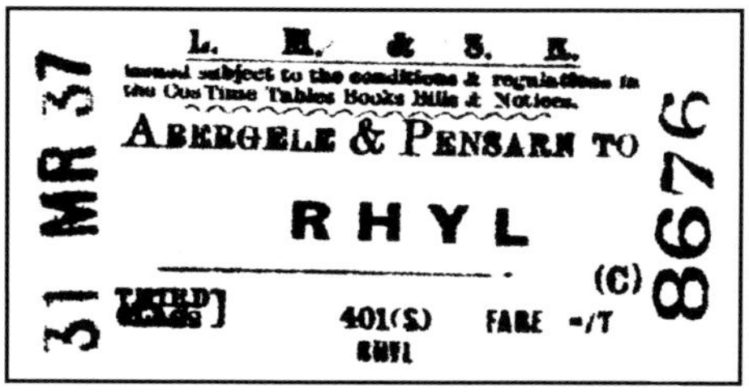

18. Provision of a road bridge in 1902 allowed a new entrance to the old building to be created at its first floor and long ramps were built down to both platforms. The roof over the down one is on the right in this 1964 photograph. (H.C.Casserley)

19. The curved footbridge gave greater clearance for the air flow above express trains. Working "wrong road" on 4th July 1965 is class 5 4-6-0 no. 45263 with an up mixed freight. (Bentley coll.)

Extract from Bradshaw's Guide for 1866.
(Reprinted by Middleton Press 2011)

ABERGELE.

POPULATION, 3,308.

Telegraph station at Rhyl, 4¼ miles

HOTEL.—The Bee (see view), Mrs. Clarke, is the best house; has very good accommodation for visitors, and can be well recommended. There are pleasure grounds connected with the house, which is within easy walking distance from the shore.

MARKET DAY.—Saturday.

FAIRS.—Feb. 12th, April 2nd, day before Holy Thursday, June 18th, October 9th. and Dec. 6th.

This station is close to the sea side, and at a little distance from the town. Its situation is very beautiful, the Clwydian range of hills forming a most picturesque and varied back ground to it; and *Gwrych Castle*, the elegant seat of Lloyd Bamford Hesketh, Esq., adding a peculiar charm to the whole. It consists of only one wide street, but the salubrity of the air, and its sea shore, render it a favourite watering place for bathing. The scenery in the neighbourhood is magnificent, and is adorned with gentlemen's seats and thickly-wooded parks. In the vicinity are British and Roman camps, Cefn Oge cave, where Richard II. lay concealed until betrayed to Bolingbroke by Percy, and the Lysfaen telegraph 709 feet high, which communicates with Liverpool.

20. Speeding west on 4th August 1979 is no. 40120, the slow line from Rhyl having been lost in September 1972. Up to six camping coaches were to be seen on a siding behind the fence on the left in earlier days. Campers had direct access to the beach. The 1902 signal box had 60 levers and was still in use in 2012. The up platform shelter was demolished in November 1987. (T.Heavyside)

21. A view in the other direction on 15th April 1985 features no. 25202 with the 15.38 Llandudno Junction to Walton Old Junction Speedlink service. The footbridge and covered ramps had gone, but part of the original building remained, beyond the signal box. (P.D.Shannon)

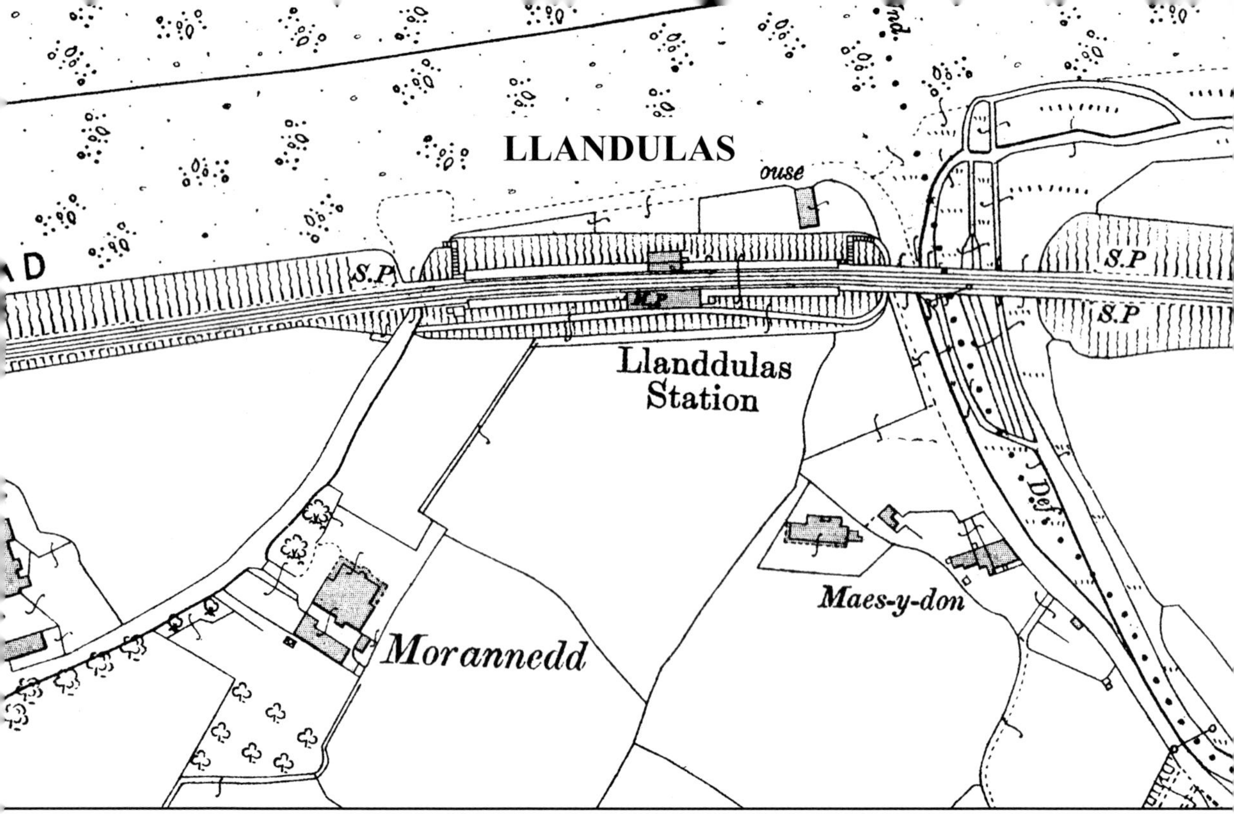

VIII. This is the 1913 edition, which was produced two years before the quadrupling from Abergele to Llandulas Viaduct. The station was open from 1st July 1889 to 1st December 1952, but it had no goods facilities.

22. Few stations offered direct access to the beach, so this location was the ideal subject for a postcard. Built entirely of wood, the entire station was destroyed by fire in 1913. (A.Dudman coll.)

LLYSFAEN

23. The station was recorded on a postcard before it closed on 5th January 1931. Much of the output of the works was used as a flux in steel making. (A.Dudman coll.)

24. A photograph from July 1948 features no. 5601 *British Guiana* working hard with a long westbound train. The signal box is in the distance. (Bentley coll.)

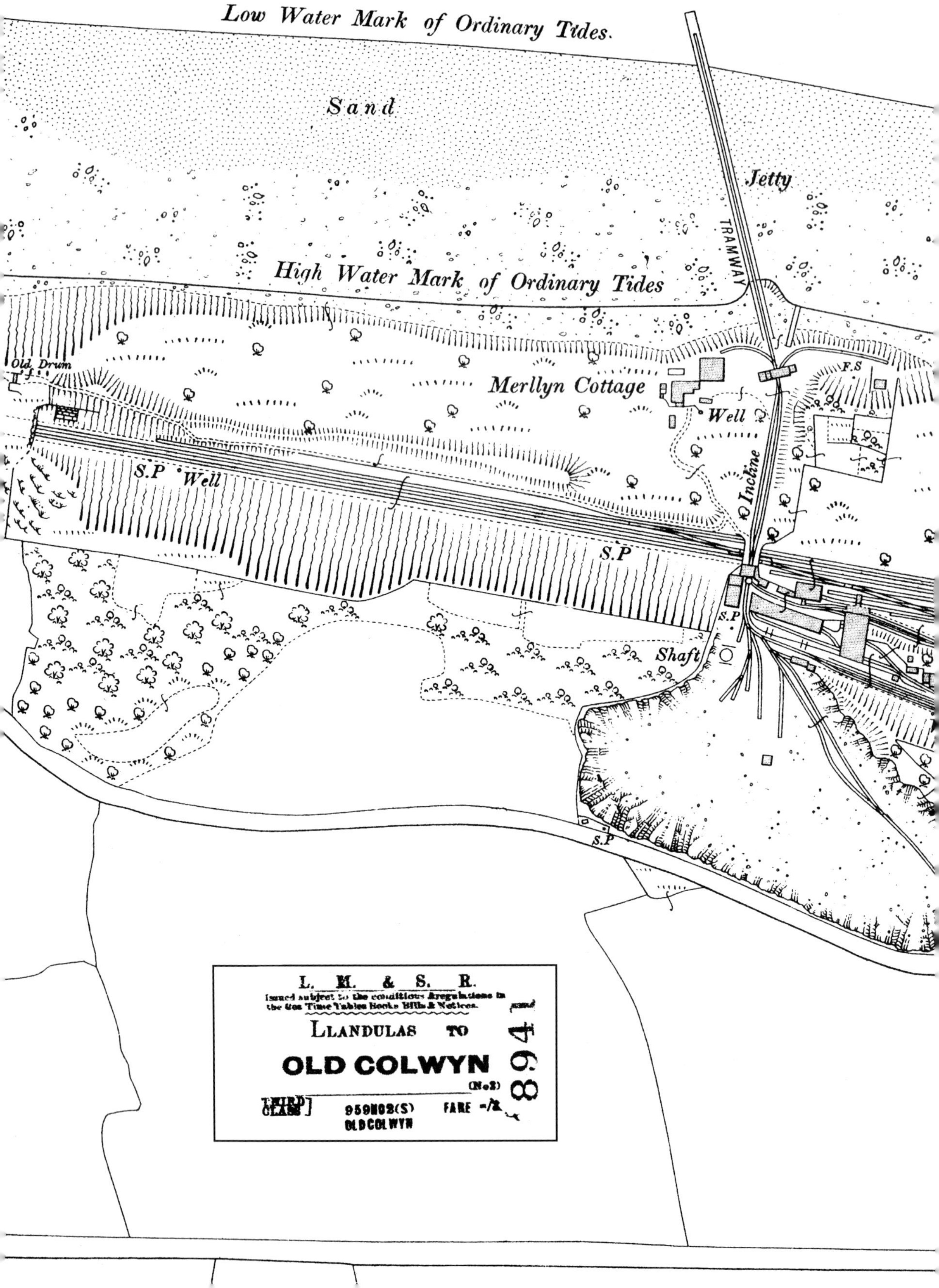
Low Water Mark of Ordinary Tides.
Sand
Jetty
TRAMWAY
High Water Mark of Ordinary Tides
Old Drum
Merllyn Cottage
Well
F.S
S.P
Well
Incline
S.P
S.P
Shaft
S.P
L. M. & S. R.
LLANDULAS TO
OLD COLWYN
(No2)
THIRD CLASS
FARE
OLD COLWYN
894

IX. This station opened on 1st August 1862 and used the name LLANDULAS until the one just seen opened in 1889. The extensive limestone quarries are shown on the 1913 edition. On the left is the east portal of Penmaenrhos Tunnel, which is 482yds long.

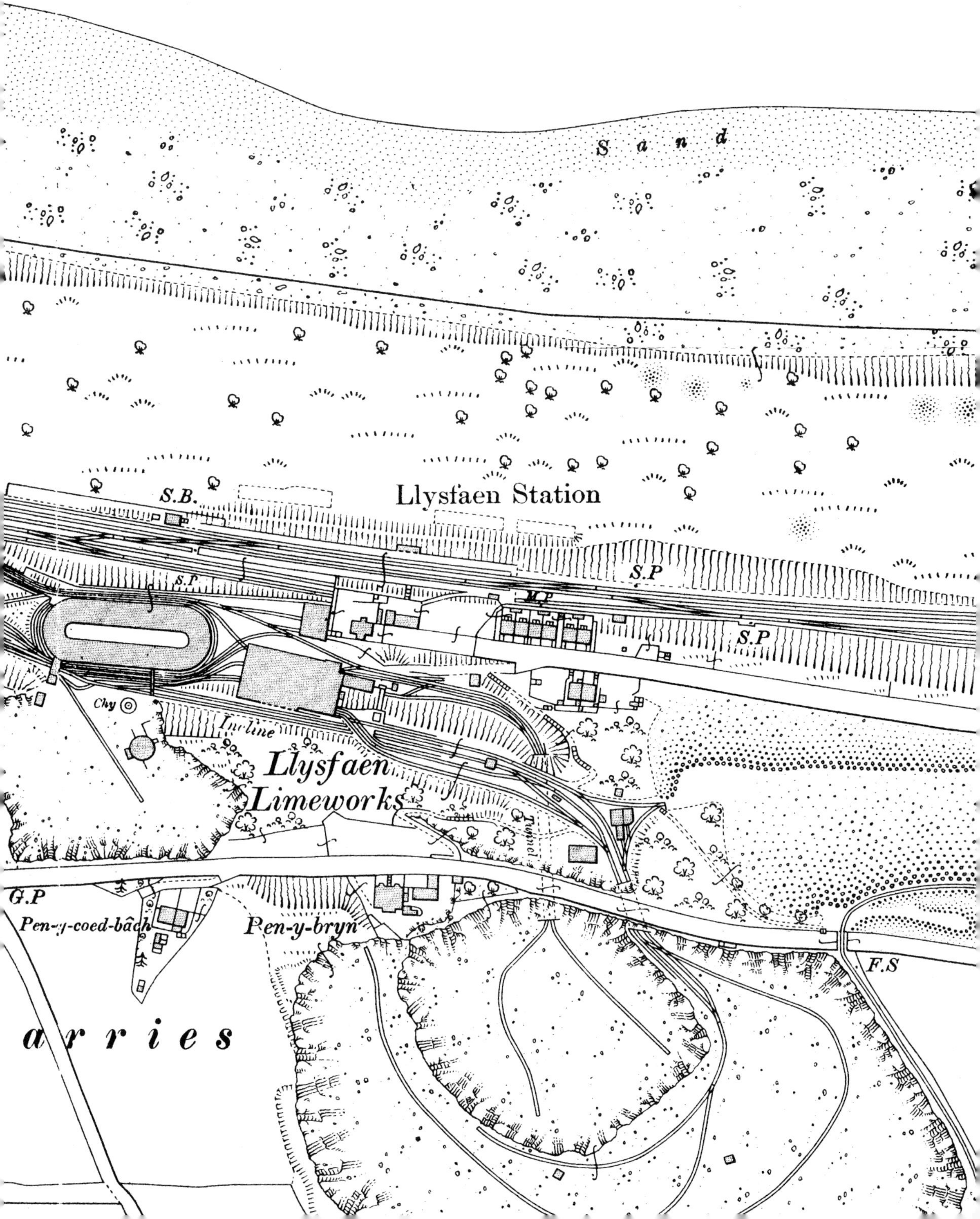

25. It is 1st September 1962 and 4-6-0 no. 46156 *The South Wales Borderer* hauls varied vans towards Rhyl. This was one of the 71 strong "Royal Scot" class. (Bentley coll.)

26. The box had a 25-lever frame and was used until 18th December 1983. It was photographed in 1962, along with its conveniently placed convenience. (Bentley coll.)

OLD COLWYN

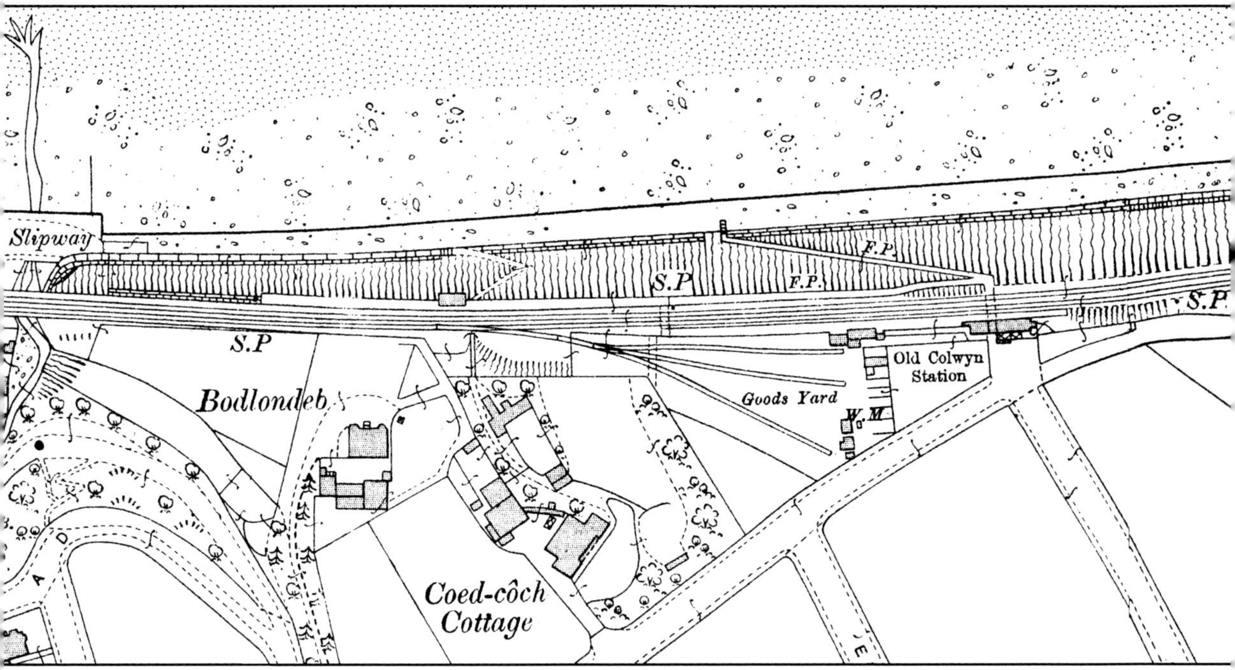

X. Another seafront station and this is shown on the 1913 edition, along with the inclined paths on the cliff down to the beach. Opening took place on 9th April 1884 and OLD was added on 22nd May 1885.

27. This eastward view has the upper floor of the main building in the distance. Its entrance was level with the subway. Closure came on 1st December 1952, but the sidings were in use until 1964. (R.M.Casserley coll.)

28. A "Precursor" class 4-4-0 is bound for Chester in about 1914. The up platform is obscured by the coaches, but the goods yard points are visible. (R.S.Carpenter coll.)

29. We are on the down platform in August 1951 and Rhos on Sea is evident. The timber walkway links the up platform with the path to the beach. The signal box had only six levers and closed on 30th May 1965. The 4-4-0 is "Compound" no. 41153. (R.G.Nelson/T.Walsh coll.)

COLWYN BAY

30. Seen east of the station is the "Irish Mail" about to collect two mail bags at speed. It may also drop one into the cage near the hut. This was an unusual subject for a postcard. (P.Q.Treloar coll.)

31. The population grew steadily and the station facilities were expanded in 1857 and 1881. A major rebuild followed in 1906-08 and the platforms were further lengthened in 1910. Approaching from the east is 2-2-2 no. 65 *Lord of the Isles*, in around 1910. (P.Q.Treloar coll.)

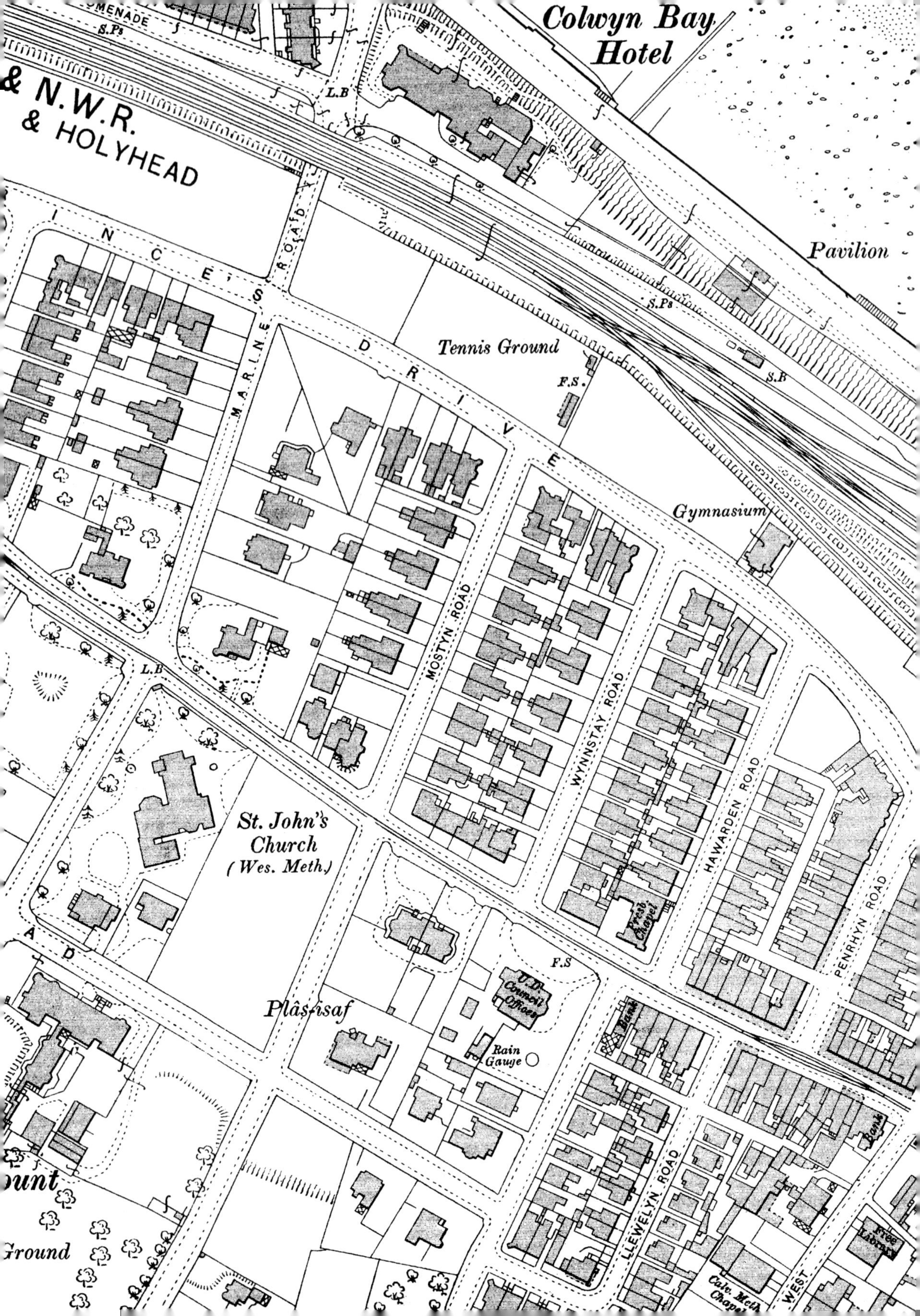
Colwyn Bay Hotel
& N.W.R.
& HOLYHEAD
Pavilion
Tennis Ground
Gymnasium
S.Ps
L.B
S.B
F.S.
MARINE ROAD
MOSTYN ROAD
WYNNSTAY ROAD
HAWARDEN ROAD
PENRHYN ROAD
LLEWELYN ROAD
WEST
St. John's Church (Wes. Meth.)
Plâs-isaf
U.D. Council Offices
Rain Gauge
Presb. Chapel
Bank
Free Library
Calv. Meth. Chapel
Ground

XI. The station opened as Colwyn in October 1849 and had Bay added on 1st August 1876. No. 1 Box is lower right on this map and it was completed in June 1904, when the quadrupled route to Llandudno Junction was ready. The goods yard was at a low level and opened on 28th March 1904. It had a 5-ton crane and closed on 4th May 1964.

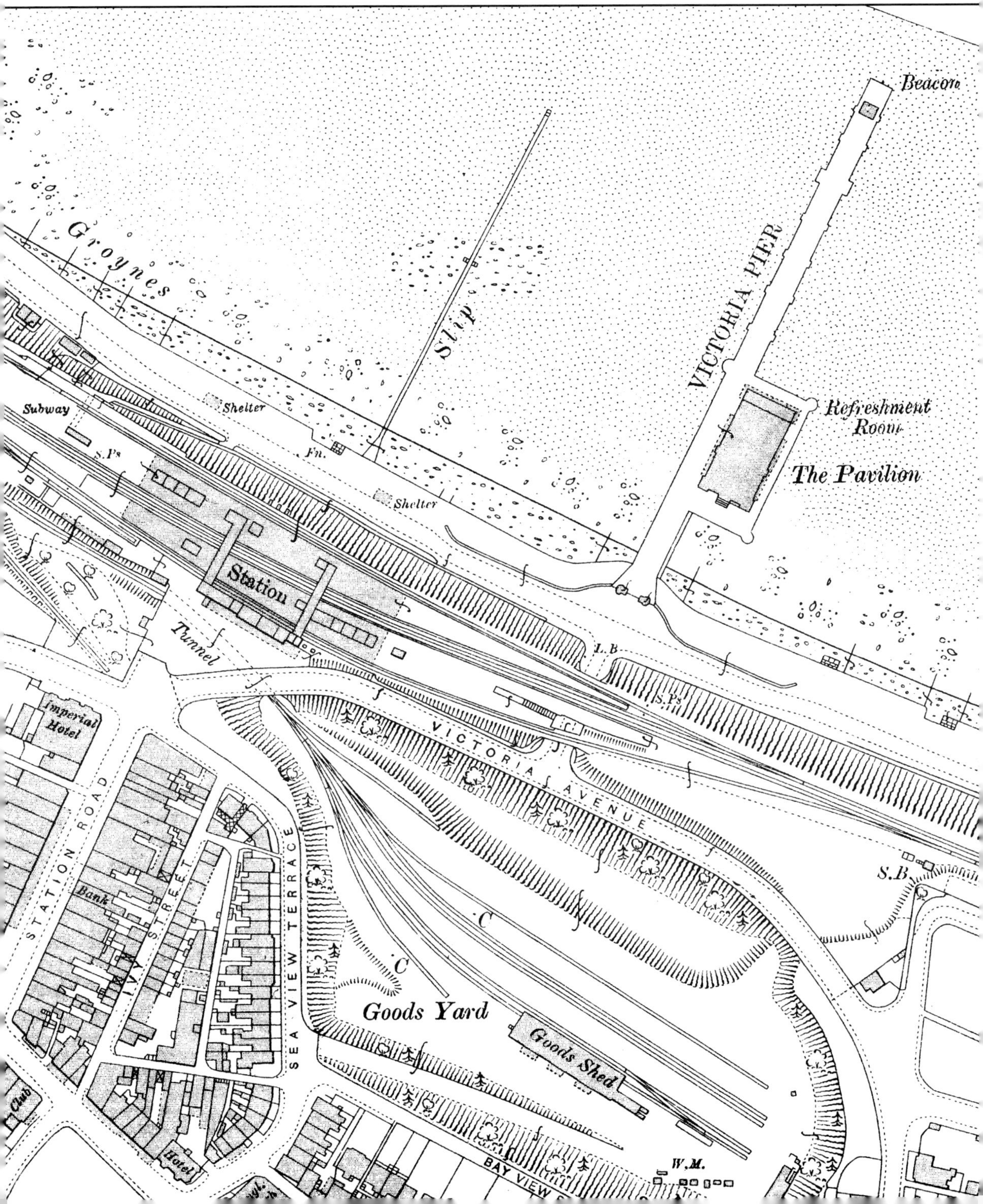

32. Entering from the west is a 4-6-0 of the "19 Inch Goods" class, probably during World War I, when there was a manpower shortage for station maintenance. (R.S.Carpenter coll.)

33. Near the right border of the map is No. 1 Box and passing it is 4-4-0 no. 41114, in about 1952. This is an LMS "3-Cylinder Compound". The box had a 20-lever frame and closed on 15th September 1968. (G.Coltas/M.J.Stretton coll.)

34. "The North Wales Land Cruise" was a very popular holiday experience in the 1950s and 2-6-0 no. 78034 is returning it to Rhyl on 23rd August 1955. Its itinery and variations were several: it always ran via Portmadoc, Barmouth and Corwen, but sometimes started at Conway or Pwllheli. (J.W.T.House/C.L.Caddy coll.)

35. The exterior was graced with a neat valence and well spaced stanchions, all intended to impress visitors. (British Railways)

36. The DMU is westbound on 4th August 1979, while no. 40028 waits to depart with the Llandudno to York service. (T.Heavyside)

37. The rear of the 15.45 Manchester Victoria to Bangor is near the 1968 signal box on 13th August 1982. No. 47104 is by the last remains of the down loop, as work began on the A55 Expressway, which was built close to the line in this area. (P.D.Shannon)

38. No. 47432 runs in with the 15.12 Llandudno to Scarborough on 6th August 1983, as road works progress on the left. The signal box had originally served at Denbigh Hall and was moved here to be opened on 15th September 1968. It had 35 levers and was closed on 2nd November 1991. (D.H.Mitchell)

39. The tower is the centre one seen in picture 36 and a plain entrance was created to the new booking hall, which opened in April 1982. The south elevation is seen on 25th May 1996, along with an interesting diversion opportunity. The A55 Expressway was built under the road in the foreground and across the site of the goods yard. (A.C.Hartless)

MOCHDRE & PABO

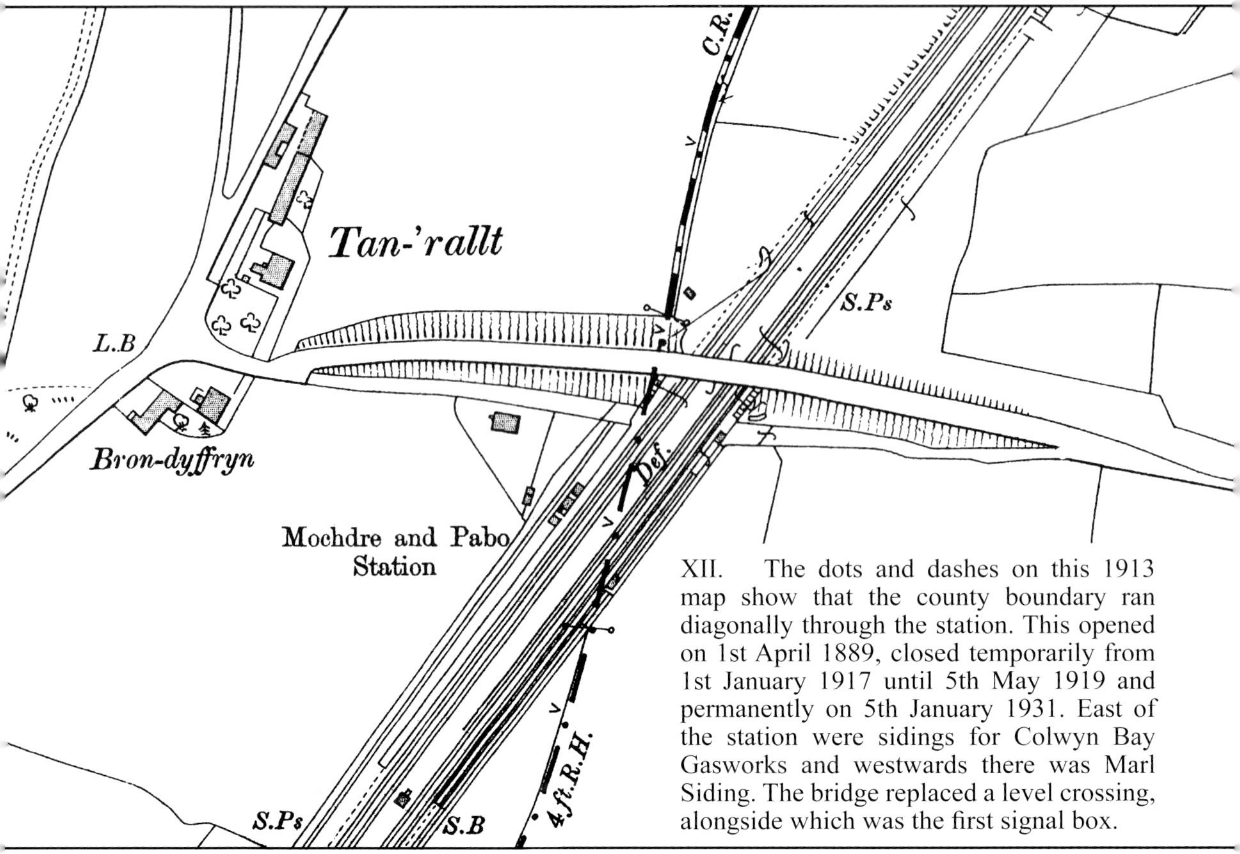

XII. The dots and dashes on this 1913 map show that the county boundary ran diagonally through the station. This opened on 1st April 1889, closed temporarily from 1st January 1917 until 5th May 1919 and permanently on 5th January 1931. East of the station were sidings for Colwyn Bay Gasworks and westwards there was Marl Siding. The bridge replaced a level crossing, alongside which was the first signal box.

40. This postcard shows the details after quadrupling in 1904. The first water troughs in the world were nearby from 1860 until 1871. The 10-lever signal box of 1904 is in the distance. From about 1930, it was only used in the Summer and it closed on 31st July 1967. The new Expressway now occupies the track site, the railway having been moved a little to the north in January 1984. Five trains called here each way in 1924. (Lens of Sutton coll.)

EAST OF LLANDUDNO JUNCTION

41. The station is in the distance as we look over the four tracks from Colwyn Bay in June 1947. In the lower left corner is the connection to the branch to Blaenau Ffestiniog, which runs up the Conway Valley. A "Jubilee" class 4-6-0 is hauling a Birmingham express and is about to pass the mail bag transfer apparatus. No. 1 Box is on the left; it had 101 levers and closed on 26th May 1968. (M.Whitehouse coll.)

42. The revised layout for branch trains is evident as no. 47459 leaves with the 09.20 Holyhead to Manchester Victoria train on 7th August 1983. This was then one of the few locations where loaded nuclear waste trains ran in both directions. The line on the right is the up passenger loop, which soon joins the up main. (D.H.Mitchell)

43. A panorama from the other side of the bridge features no. 40131 with the 07.52 Leeds to Llandudno on 24th July 1982. The siding on the right branches into three, which form the Glan Conway Freight Terminal. The points for the 1898 Conway Valley Line are under the fifth coach. The depot on the right had oil tanks and was opened in 1980 to handle coal as well. The branch junction was moved east at that time. (T.Heavyside)

LLANDUDNO JUNCTION

44. This westward panorama includes Conway Castle and shows the first station, with a short dock line close to Conway Road, which became the A55 in 1919. The down loop and its platform has an overall roof and the two footbridges appear to join one another. The locomotive is not facing a signal and so is presumably shunting. (A.Dudman coll.)

45. The new station was very spacious, with four through platforms and four bays. There was good weather protection and a wide footbridge, with luggage lifts. (Lens of Sutton coll.)

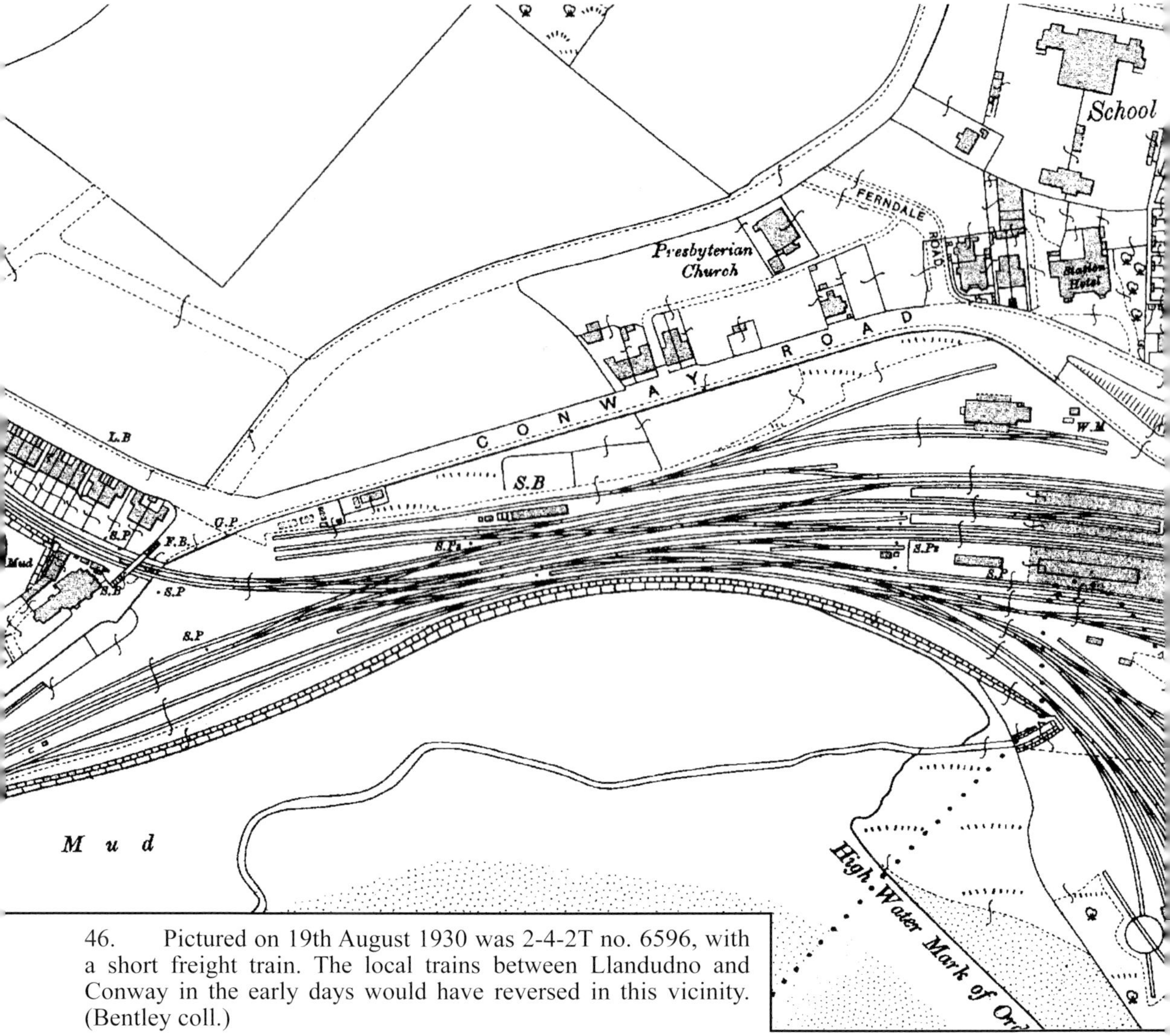

46. Pictured on 19th August 1930 was 2-4-2T no. 6596, with a short freight train. The local trains between Llandudno and Conway in the early days would have reversed in this vicinity. (Bentley coll.)

XIII. The 1898 station is across the join of the pages on this 1913 map and the branch to Llandudno curves upwards on the left. Below this had been the original station with the up main and the down branch platforms between the routes. There was a down main island platform, the Conway Valley trains using the loop. They used the line along the shore until 1897. This was then severed at its curve south to form a long siding.

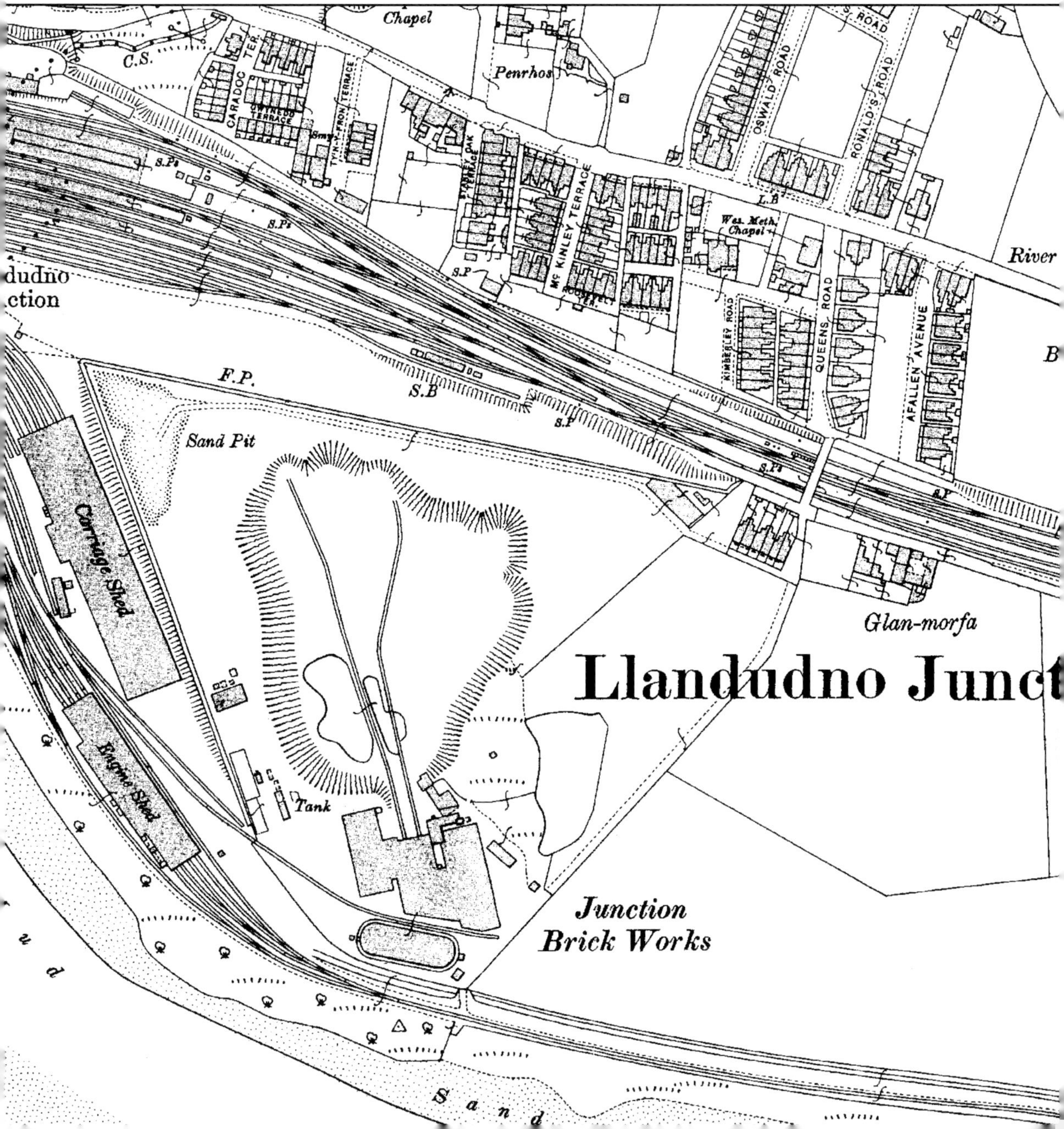

47. A Holyhead line train is departing west, sometime around 1960. No. 2 Box is on the right, overlooking the junction, which has contrasting signal posts. (J.H.Moss/R.S.Carpenter)

48. A motor train from Llandudno is being propelled into the station by a 2-6-2T in about 1963. The large building, near the rear of the train, housed bananas in vast quantities - all arrived by rail. (J.H.Moss/R.S.Carpenter)

49. The entrance is on the left in this view from 29th August 1964. The towers house the luggage lifts and platform 1 is beyond the left building. A spacious bus inter-exchange was created later, on the right. (H.C.Casserley)

50. No. 1 Box is in the right background in this view of 2-6-0 no. 42727 with immaculate buffers. To the right of the train is a windscreen; the original station also had one. The train ran from Birmingham Snow Hill on 20th March 1966 and terminated here. (Bentley coll.)

51. This view is from the footbridge on the left of the map and has one of the two goods sheds visible between the signal box (154 levers) and the banana warehouse. The puddles are on the site of the original branch up platform. The level crossing was replaced by a bridge in 1968. (Bentley coll.)

52. The first engine shed housed 12 locomotives and was completed in 1879. It was doubled in size in 1898 and is seen on 25th June 1966. There were 38 locomotives listed here as late as 1958, when the code was 6G. Closure came in 1966. (H.C.Casserley)

53. The carriage shed is marked on the map and it lasted just over 100 years, being demolished in 2000. It was photographed in July 1982, when used for DMUs. Their oil tank is in the centre of the view, between two class 25s and no. 40002. (T.Heavyside)

54. The DMU at platform 3 on 6th August 1983 is forming the 15.15 Holyhead to Llandudno. There were five such trains reversing here on weekdays at that period. Platform 4 (centre) was little used and the one on the left had only a siding nearby. The grass is on the site of the bays for Conway Valley trains. (D.H.Mitchell)

55. Platform 2 is on the right, but No. 3 is obscured by tankers from Amlwch on Anglesey on 15th April 1985. The grey ones contain ethylene dibromide and the white ones chlorine. They are bound for Ellesmere Port, but they will first have to be reversed out of the station to regain the main line. The remnant of the platform 4 canopy is near the rear of the train. (P.D.Shannon)

For other pictures of this area, please see nos 101 to 109 in our *Bala to Llandudno* album.

56. No. 175009 waits to start its short journey to Llandudno at 16.04 from platform 2 on 6th September 2009. This was the only bay platform remaining in use by that time. (V.Mitchell)

57. Our final view of the junction is from an open top bus on the same day. We are on the bridge which replaced the level crossing; the signal box (centre) was opened on 9th February 1985. It was fitted with a panel. (V.Mitchell)

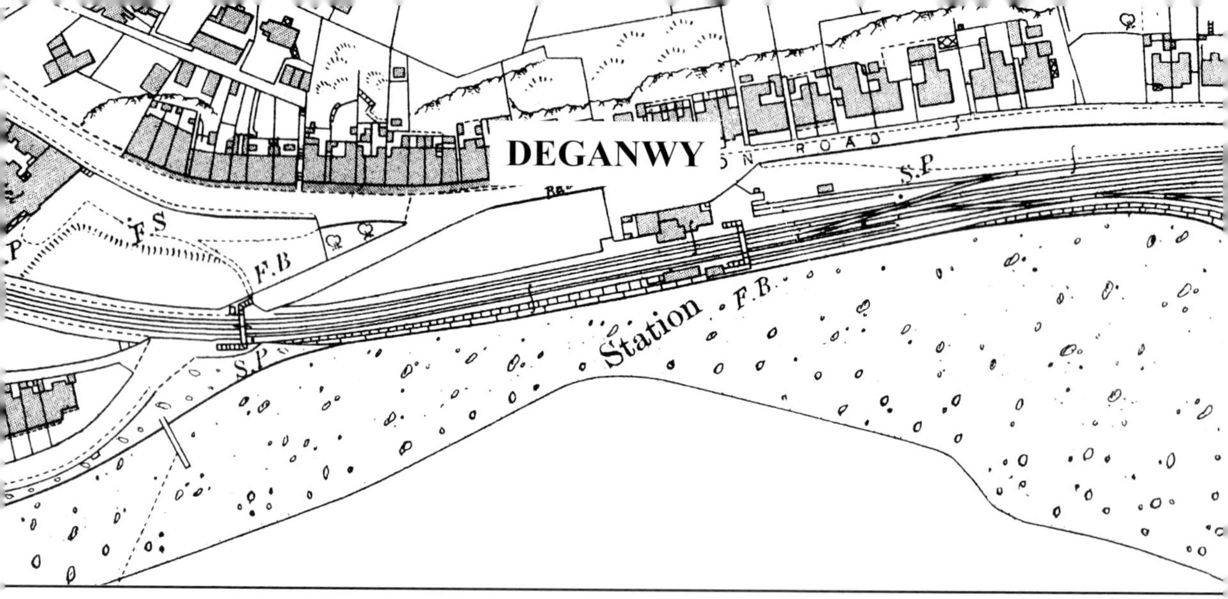

XIV. The 1912 edition shows that the pier had a complex of narrow gauge tracks, as 2ft gauge loaded slate wagons came from Blaenau Ffestiniog and were unloaded from transporter wagons. Each of these carried four small wagons. The pier was created in 1882 from waste rock.

58. Although the branch was leased by the LNWR from 1862, the station was not opened until 1st June 1866. This view is from the left of the right page and has the station in the distance. On the right is No. 1 Box, which was in use from March 1884 to May 1967. It had 26 levers. One wagon is standing in the small goods yard, which closed on 7th September 1964. (J.Woods)

➔ 59. The goods shed is included in this view from about 1949. Few named trains were pushed and were devoid of corridors. Not stopping at Llandudno Junction, the destination would be Rhyl or Prestatyn. The points on the right gave access to the pier, which was a commercial failure. Most Blaenau slate was shipped to destinations in the south and so it was conveyed by the Festiniog Railway to the harbour at Portmadoc, to use the contemporary spellings. (M.J.Stretton coll.)

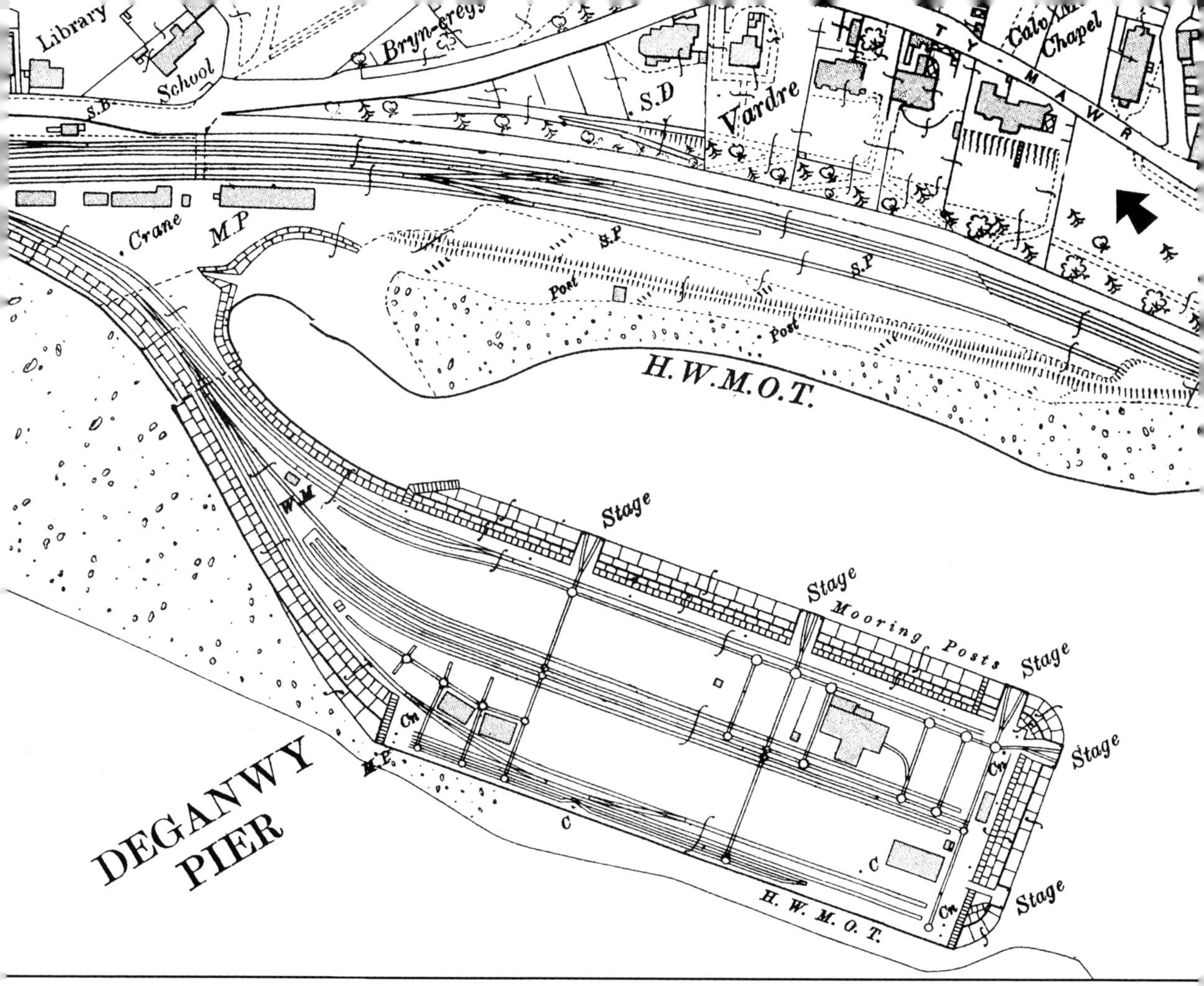
Library
School
Bryn-ereys
S.D
Vardre
Calo M Chapel
TY MAWR
S.B
Crane
M.P
S.P
Post
H.W.M.O.T.
Stage
W.M
Mooring Posts
Cn
M.P
C
DEGANWY PIER

41211
THE WELSH DRAGON

60. The reason for this unusual view may have been to record a romantic encounter. The massive footbridge above 4-6-0 no. 73044 was probably necessary due to prolonged gate closure caused by shunting empty coaches on and off the pier. There was a use for it after all: stock storage. (R.S.Carpenter coll.)

61. The 17.14 Llandudno to Derby arrives on 25th July 1990, when No. 2 Box of 1914 had lost its number. The 18-lever frame was still in use in 2012, but the gates had gone in favour of barriers. The dragon was painted red. (T.Heavyside)

62. This and the next photograph were taken on 6th September 2009. An earlier view of this crossing is to be seen in picture 58. The old slate wharves on the pier were adapted to accommodate a stylish housing development. New highways seldom appear with barriers, close to a road junction. The bay east of the pier was infilled to enlarge Deganwy Quay, as it is known locally. (V.Mitchell)

Other views of this station can be found in pictures 110 to 113 in *Bala to Llandudno*.

63. The elegant, historic buildings were destroyed in about 1996 and were replaced by bus shelters. It is clear that the signal box operator has a direct line of sight to the new level crossing behind the camera. (V.Mitchell)

LLANDUDNO

XV. The branch was double from 1st June 1876 and the popularity of the town grew rapidly. There were initially only two platforms. The 1912 map shows the extent of the station completed in 1903 and that the goods shed shared its southeast wall. The long siding curving through a gate served the gasworks, until its closure in 1956. The goods yard closed on 3rd April 1967, but coal traffic continued until 31st May 1976. The turntable was 60ft long.

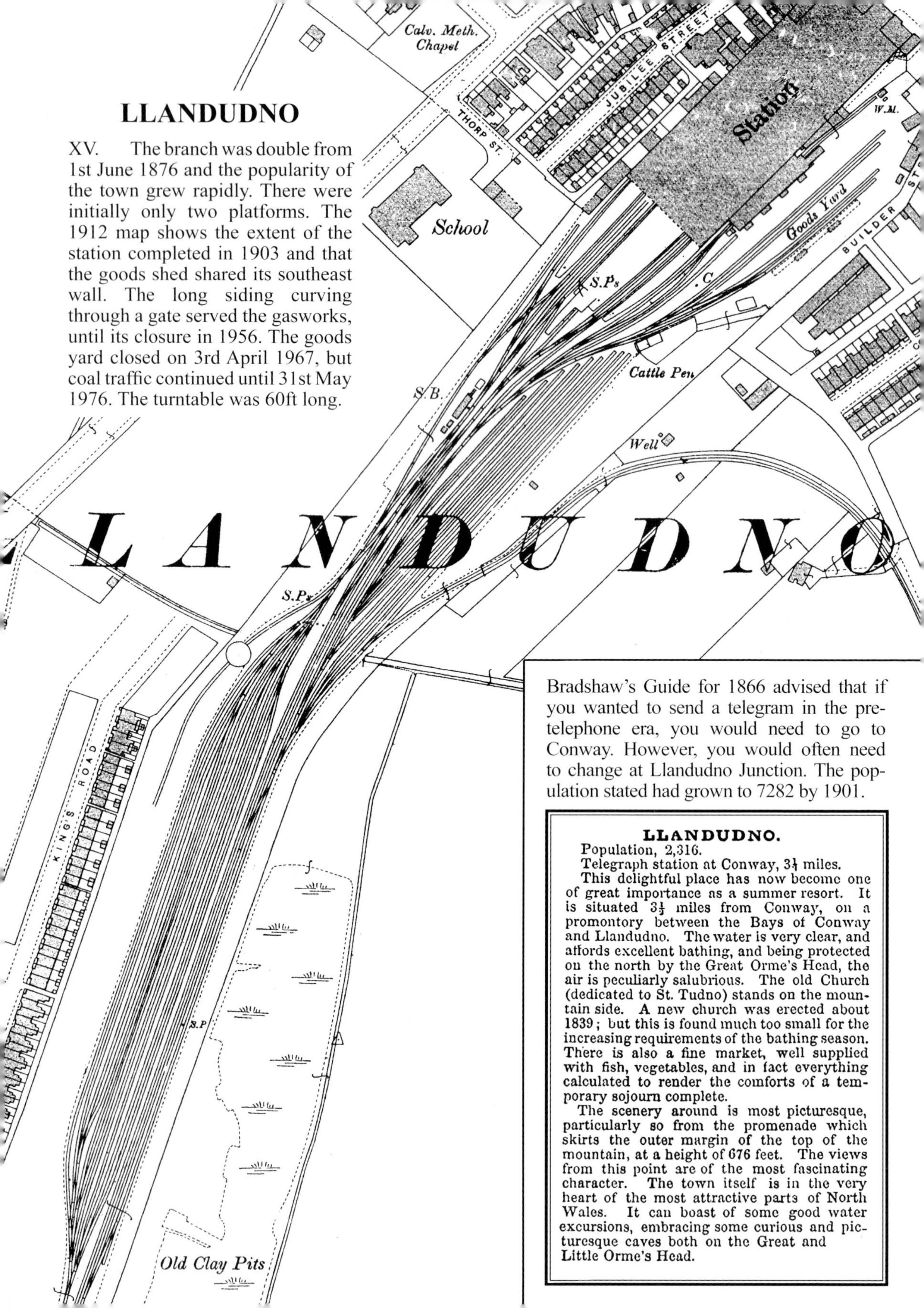

Bradshaw's Guide for 1866 advised that if you wanted to send a telegram in the pre-telephone era, you would need to go to Conway. However, you would often need to change at Llandudno Junction. The population stated had grown to 7282 by 1901.

LLANDUDNO.

Population, 2,316.

Telegraph station at Conway, 3¼ miles.

This delightful place has now become one of great importance as a summer resort. It is situated 3½ miles from Conway, on a promontory between the Bays of Conway and Llandudno. The water is very clear, and affords excellent bathing, and being protected on the north by the Great Orme's Head, the air is peculiarly salubrious. The old Church (dedicated to St. Tudno) stands on the mountain side. A new church was erected about 1839; but this is found much too small for the increasing requirements of the bathing season. There is also a fine market, well supplied with fish, vegetables, and in fact everything calculated to render the comforts of a temporary sojourn complete.

The scenery around is most picturesque, particularly so from the promenade which skirts the outer margin of the top of the mountain, at a height of 676 feet. The views from this point are of the most fascinating character. The town itself is in the very heart of the most attractive parts of North Wales. It can boast of some good water excursions, embracing some curious and picturesque caves both on the Great and Little Orme's Head.

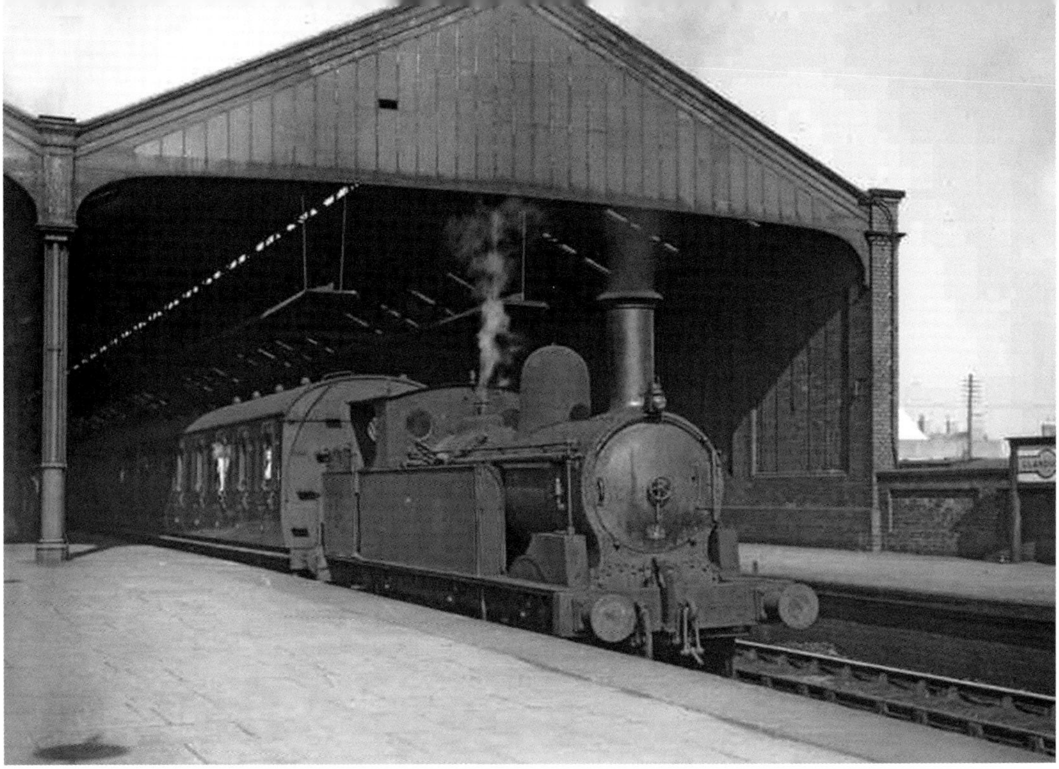

64. No details survive of this fine record of a "Coal Tank" 0-6-2T at platform 2, when the roof was still complete with smoke deflectors. This was a typical local train in the 1950s and is probably bound for the Conway Valley. (Milepost 92½)

65. BR 2-6-2Ts were common in the 1960s and no. 84001 stands with corridor stock forming the Llandudno portion of "The Welshman". It would join the sections from Holyhead and Portmadoc at Llandudno Junction. The new station was built between 1892 and 1903. (R.S.Carpenter coll.)

66. The roof was dismantled in stages and this is the scene on 30th September 1969. All platforms were still usable, although few long trains were using them by that time. However, a direct London service was operated again between September 2004 and December 2008. (R.F.Roberts/SLS coll.)

67. Under the residue of the roof on 17th June 1989 is class 117 DMU no. T305, which is in GWR livery as part of the 150th anniversary celebrations of that company. (B.I.Nathan)

↓ 68. An unwelcoming sight greeted passengers for decades and the scene on 6th September 2009 was almost unchanged when visited two years later. South hereof, a new bridge for Maesdu Road opened on 9th September 2010. (V.Mitchell)

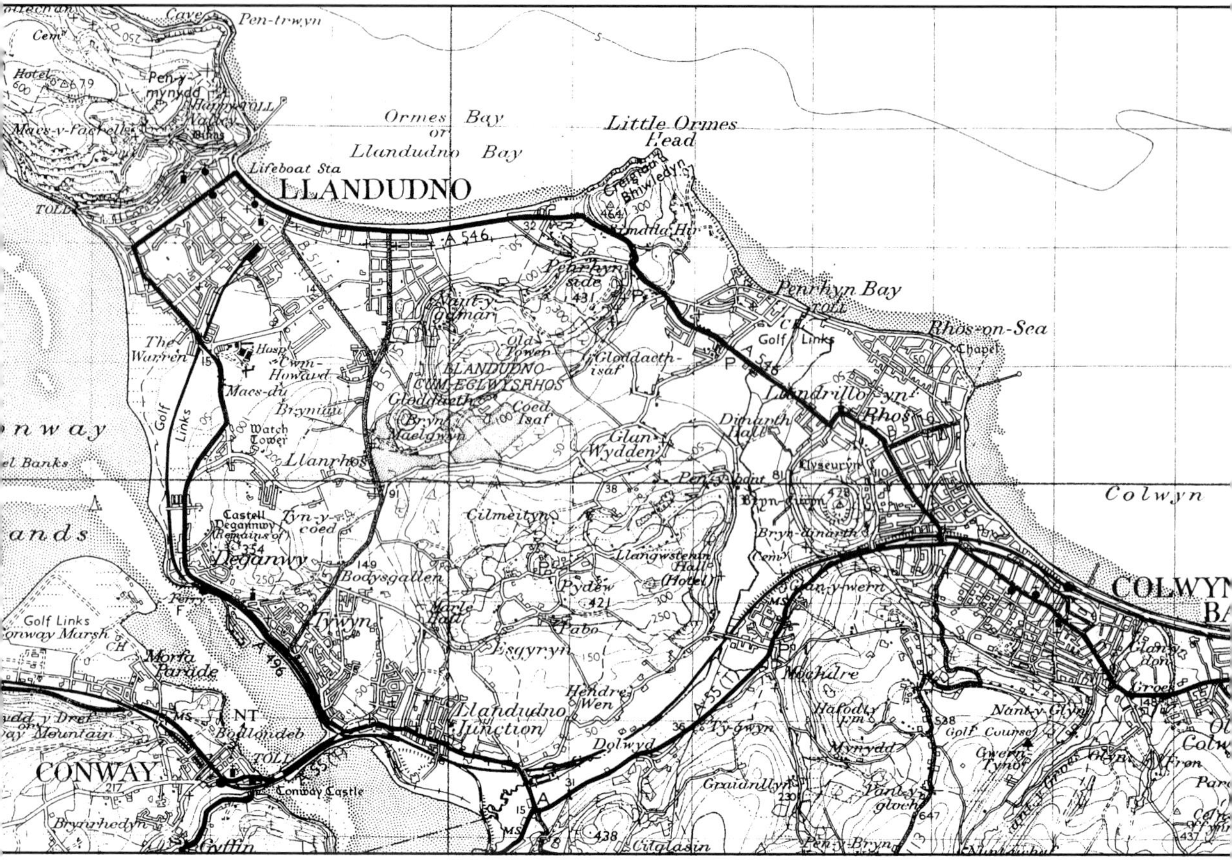

XVI. The 1953 edition at 1 inch to 1 mile reveals that Deganwy still had a ferry and shows the long waterfront siding south of Llandudno Junction. Small sections of non-highway track also appear. One is included in the *Llandudno & Colwyn Bay Tramway* album and the western one was part of the Great Orme Tramway, which is still cable operated. The former was in use in 1907-56.

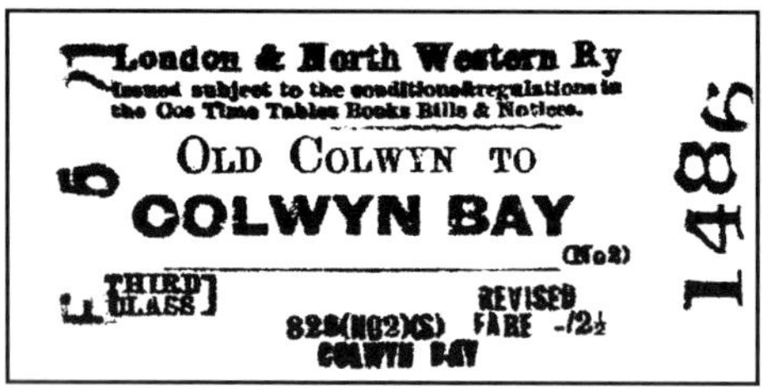

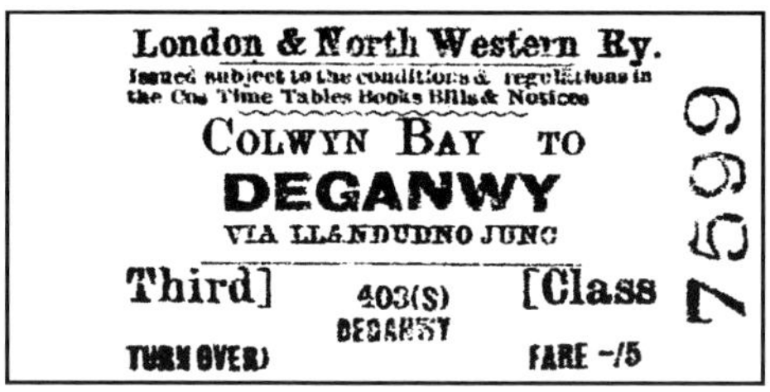

Further illustrations of this important terminus are numbered 114 onwards in *Bala to Llandudno.*

69. The signal box was still in use when photographed on 30th November 2011, its frame having 86 levers. It was termed No. 2 until 13th September 1970, when No. 1 closed. This had 15 levers and was at the south end of the carriage sidings, just off the map. No. 175101 is working the 09.45 to Manchester Piccadilly. (L.Davies)

70. This photograph of the 07.50 from Manchester Piccadilly on the same day gives a rare glimpse of the crossover between No. 1 and No. 2 roads, by that time little used; neither were the four carriage sidings. Work was due to start on a transport exchange on the abandoned area on the right. (L.Davies)

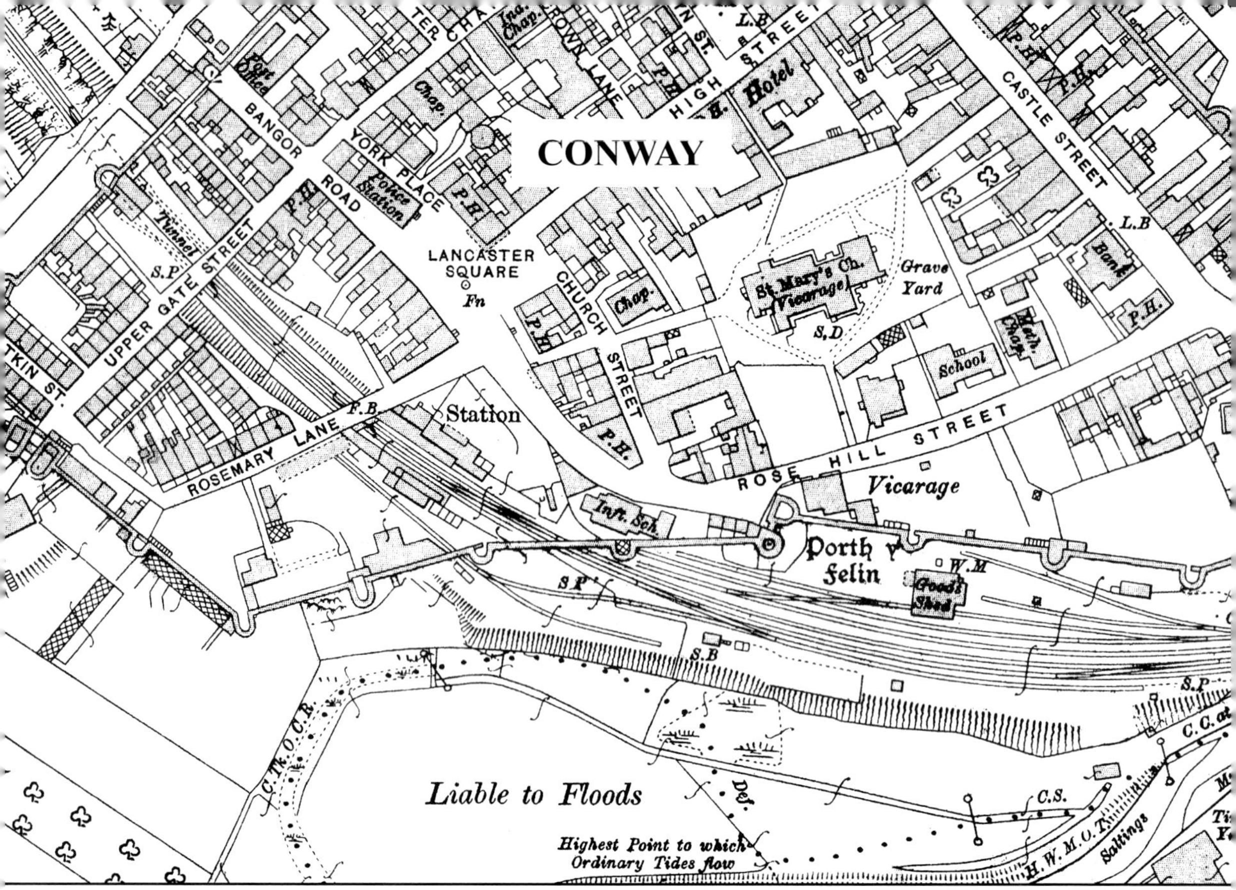

71. The station opened on 1st May 1848 although the first tube of the bridge came into use on 18th April of that year. The bridge span for Rosemary Lane is immediately beyond the footbridge. The road had originally been carried on a stone arch. The photograph is from about 1955 and in the background is the 74yd long Conway Tunnel. (Lens of Sutton coll.)

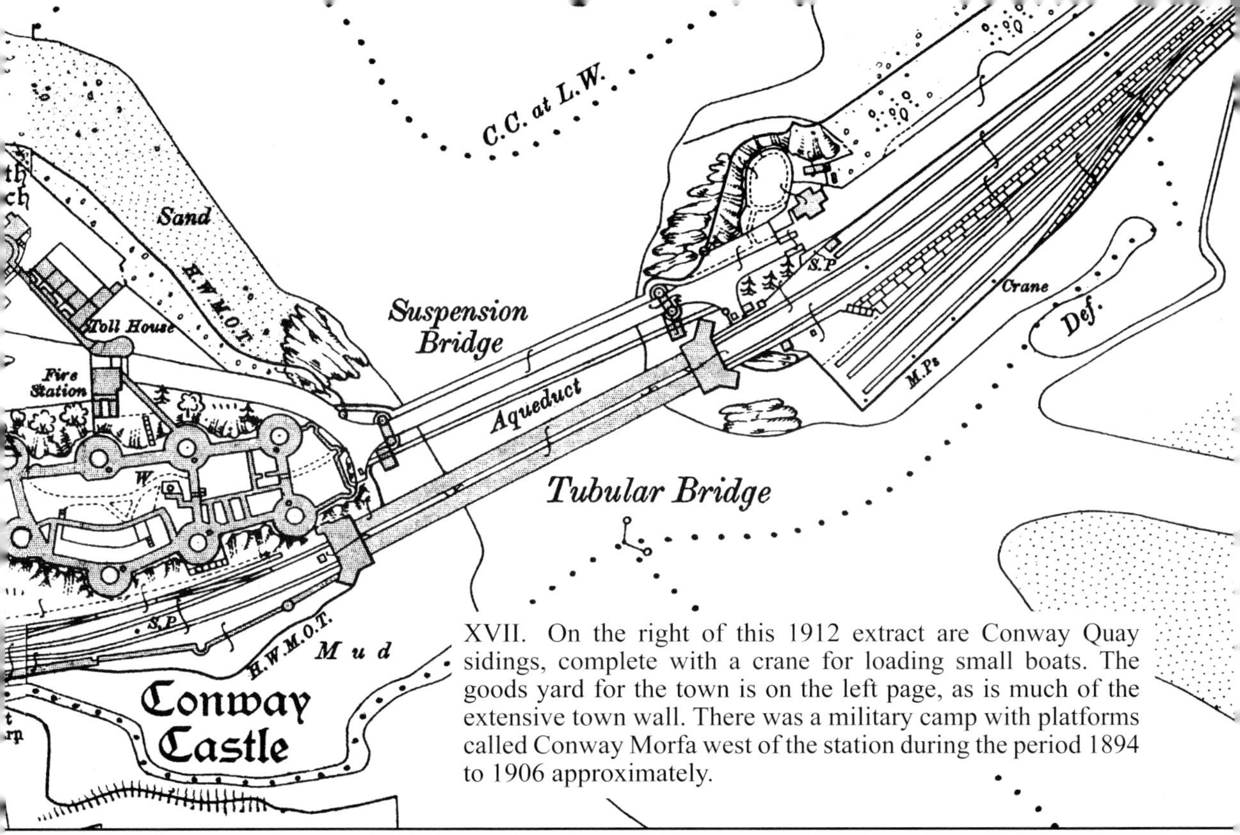

XVII. On the right of this 1912 extract are Conway Quay sidings, complete with a crane for loading small boats. The goods yard for the town is on the left page, as is much of the extensive town wall. There was a military camp with platforms called Conway Morfa west of the station during the period 1894 to 1906 approximately.

72. The railway builders respected the town's history and created an arch in the town wall, complete with battlements. These continue in the left background of this picture from 4th July 1957. No. 45110, an ex-LMS 4-6-0, is waiting to depart alongside the goods yard. The siding on the left ran through the wall into the Signal Department's yard. (Bentley coll.)

73. The station had been fire damaged in 1858, enlarged in 1861 and again in 1875. The unusual stanchions protect the personal weighing machine at the foot of the steps. Looking east in 1962, we see the 25-lever signal box, which was closed on 7th September 1968. It was demolished by the engineers in May 1969, using conflagration. (D.K.Jones coll.)

74. The towers at each end of Stephenson's Tubular Bridge complemented Conway Castle with multiple battlements. The passing of a down express on 6th August 1964 does not seem to distract those on the bowling green. The train will soon run through Conway station and then pass Conway Morfa signal box, which was only manned when access was required to the siding used for wood and scrap traffic. This ceased in 1966 and the box was demolished in July 1967. (D.Johnson)

75. A rare view from one of the bridge towers features an up "Irish Mail" passing the constricted goods yard, which was open until 5th March 1964. In use is the 5-ton crane, which was still standing in 2012. (British Railways)

76. The main building was on the north side, close to the town square. Passenger service ceased on 14th February 1966 and the photograph was taken soon after. The impending development of tourism was not appreciated by many at that time. The town lost its A in 1971. (J.Woods)

CONWY

77. The station was rebuilt and opened again on 29th June 1987. A Pacer (or "Skipper") forming a Bangor to Llandudno Junction service arrives on 30th June 1988. Each car had only four wheels and so was best suited to coastal routes and not steep gradients. (D.K.Jones coll.)

78. From the south, the age of the stonework of the castle contrasts with that of the railway engineers. A class 150 DMU formed the 09.40 Wakefield Westgate to Holyhead service on 25th July 1990. The brick buttress behind the train toilet was provided by the LNWR in 1881. (T.Heavyside)

79. The goods yard had been on the right of this picture, which features HST no. 43128 working the 13.55 from Holyhead to Euston on 11th October 1991. These reliable and popular units operated this service until May 2004. (T.Heavyside)

80. The span of the tubes (right) was reduced from 400 to 310 feet in 1899, by adding new supporting cylinders. Two are seen in picture 74. Centre is the suspension bridge created by Telford and opened in 1826. The crossing of the A55 Expressway cannot be seen, as it is inside tubes sunk onto the river bed. An HST is forming the 14.13 Holyhead to Euston on 11th April 1999 and is seen from the top of the castle. On the left is the new bridge carrying the A547. (P.G.Barnes)

PENMAENMAWR

XVIII. The 1913 edition is fascinating as it reveals the diverse activities from granite loading to up market leisure provision. At least seven places of worship are shown, plus an esplanade and a promenade.

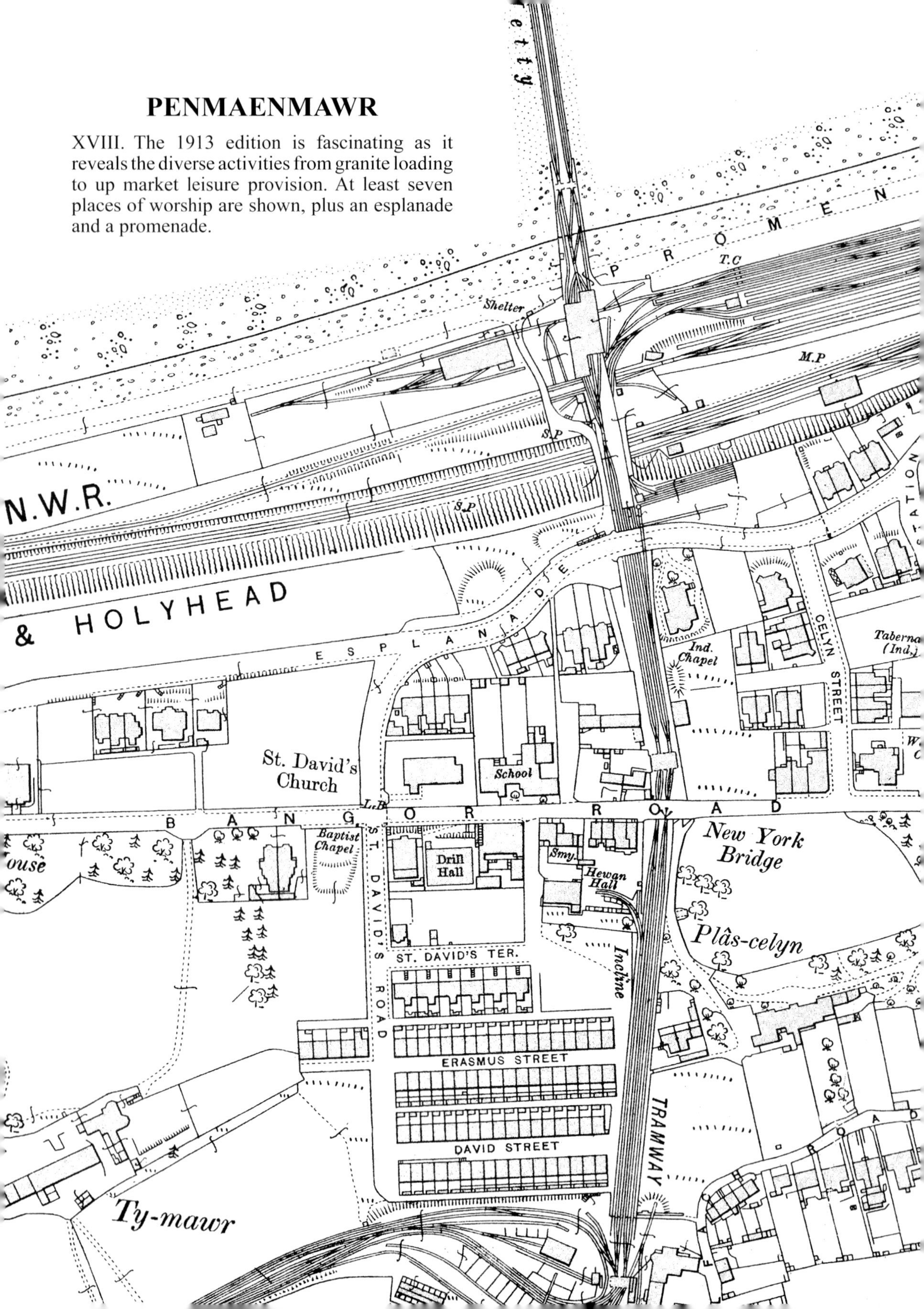

Stage
Shelter
E
S.P
S.P
STATION ROAD EAST
S.P
S.B
F.B
L.B Station
W.M
WEST
Fn
CONSTITUTION HILL
PARADISE ROAD
CONWA
BRYNMOR TERRACE
Grand Hotel
Fn
F.B.
W.M
Monument
P.H.
L.B
Oxford Hall
PANT-YR-AFON
M.S
Hotel
Bank
Fn
Bank
Post Office
Congregational Chapel
Calv. Meth. Chapel
English Presb. Church
FERNBROO
F.P.
F.S
G.P
F.P.

81. This view over the town is from the west and is from a district known as Penmaenan. It is in the background of the next photograph; both are late Victorian. The station opened in October 1849. (R.S.Carpenter coll.)

82. A westward panorama shows little development between the station and the beach. Much of this land would be used for the many sidings shown on the map and in later photographs. They were laid in 1888, when the pier was replaced. (R.S.Carpenter coll.)

83. The arrival of a stopping train for Bangor was recorded on 24th August 1937. The locomotive is no. 8485, an ex-LNWR "Cauliflower" class 0-6-0. The building was not original, but was of the style seen elsewhere. (R.S.Carpenter coll.)

84. This was part of an LMS poster and it seems to have two nuns admiring a Thornycroft lorry and one tennis player doing likewise to his partner. The granite outcrop in the background gives its name to the town. Access to the beach is behind the lorry. Some of the granite workings (top left) were photographed in the 1930s. Most of the output was for road making or railway ballast. The census recorded 3780 residents in 1961. The quarry began in 1830 and produced only setts until 1896, but this ceased in the 1930s. The first crushing plant came in 1893. (British Railways)

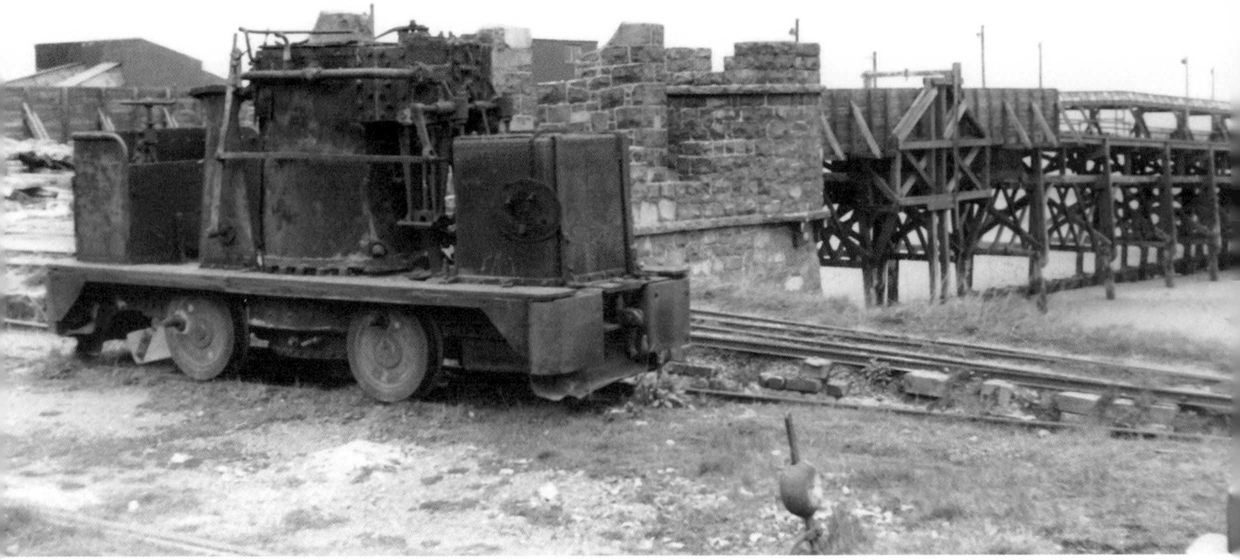

85. Part of the 3ft gauge system was recorded on 16th April 1965 at a time when conveyor belts were the main means of quarry transport. Long out of use was *Watkin*, which had been built by de Winton in Carnarvon in 1893 and was later preserved at Dinas Junction. The lines went out of use in about 1967. (A.Neale)

86. We now have three photographs from 25th July 1990. This features no. 31158 ready to leave with a ballast train. The A55 Expressway changed the seafront of the town for ever and required a tunnel through the headland. A ledge had been cut into it for an improved road in 1936. Until 1772, the road was only usable at low tide. (T.Heavyside)

87. The container train is bound for Holyhead behind no. 47354 and near the rear wagon is the signal box, which opened on 13th December 1952 with 25 levers. It was still in use in 2012, but container traffic ceased in March 1991. The first box had been to the left of the camera until 1950. Its successor was built where seen, following a major accident on 27th August 1950, when the up "Irish Mail" collided at 3.0am with an engine shunting. Six died. (T.Heavyside)

88. No. 150213 is working the 13.56 Bangor to Llandudno and is passing a ballast train. The goods yard had been on the left and was open until 4th May 1964. A new stone hopper of 5000 ton capacity came into use on 16th October 1984. The platforms take eight coaches each. (T.Heavyside)

89. Nos 37379 and 37799 wait in the loading siding on 26th October 1998, ready to depart for Manchester Guide Bridge. By 2010, there were only one or two trains per week. The new tunnel and old highway ledge are clearer in this view. (P.D.Shannon)

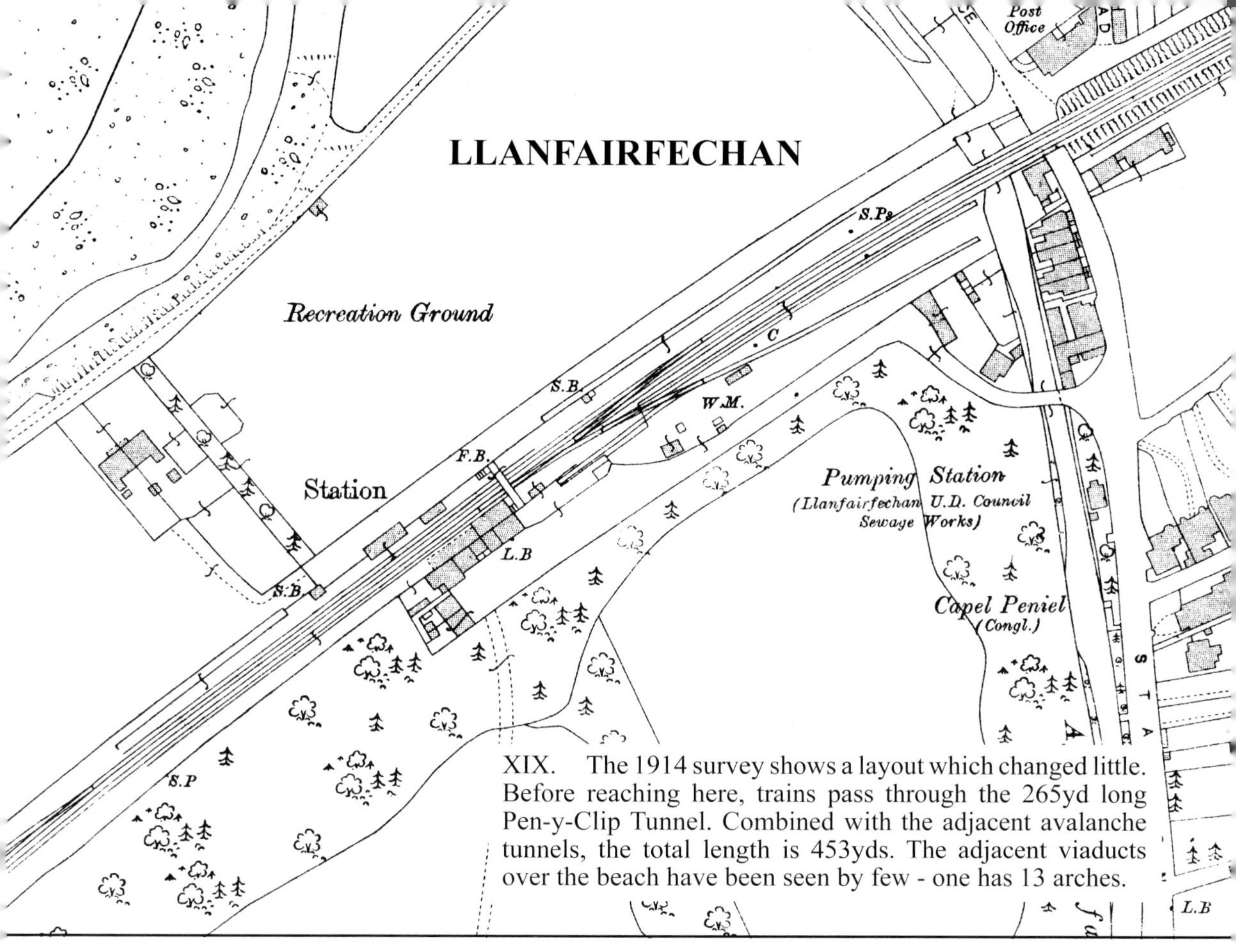

XIX. The 1914 survey shows a layout which changed little. Before reaching here, trains pass through the 265yd long Pen-y-Clip Tunnel. Combined with the adjacent avalanche tunnels, the total length is 453yds. The adjacent viaducts over the beach have been seen by few - one has 13 arches.

90. An eastward view in about 1935 shows no light behind the glass. Often the oil lamps were put in place at dusk. The station opened after most, on 1st May 1860. The local population was a little under 3000 for the first half of the 20th century. (Stations UK)

91. Leaving for Chester on 19th July 1941 is 4-4-0 no. 1123, one of a class of 195 such engines. On the left is the goods yard, which received a small shed in 1865 and closed on 1st June 1964. (H.C.Casserley)

92. A wider view from 12th August 1953 includes a Hawkseye nameboard, a type widely used by the LMS. It seems that gas lighting with shadowless bowls had arrived by that time. (H.C.Casserley)

93. This 1964 record is from the footbridge and includes the connection to the goods yard. The signal box had an 18-lever frame and was used until 27th August 1967. The facilities for gentlemen included a roof. (Stations UK)

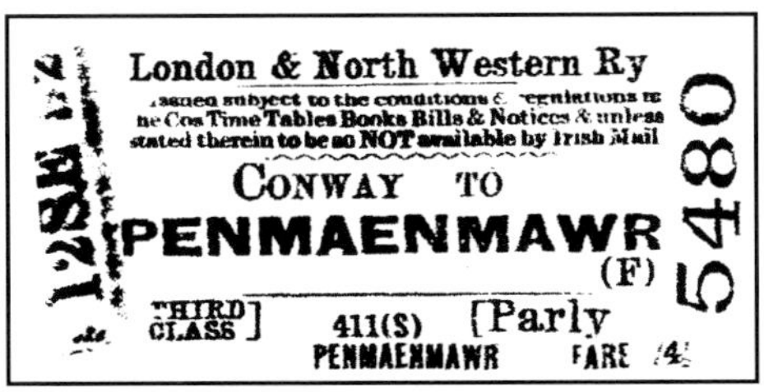

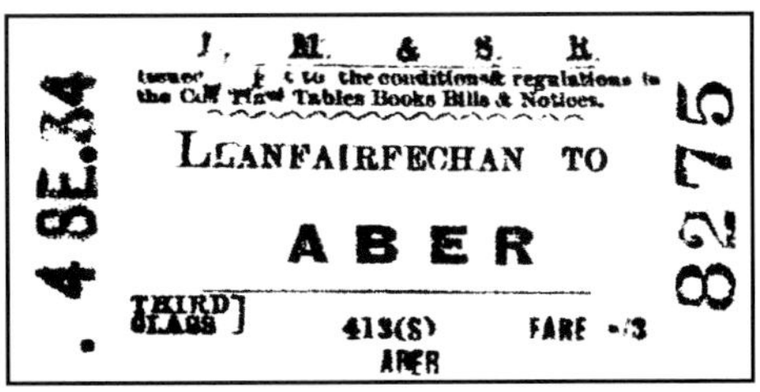

94. This 5.02pm Llandudno Junction to Holyhead was hauled by 4-6-0 no. 44770 on 28th August 1964. It is passing the retired signal box, which explains why two are shown on the map. Retirement took place in 1889. (H.C.Casserley)

95. Virgin Voyager no. 221103 speeds through forming the 08.10 Euston to Holyhead on 31st October 2011. All but the footbridge was destroyed to accommodate the Expressway, which is behind the wall on the right. Penmaen Mawr rises to over 1000ft on the right. Demolition of the buildings had taken place in March 1988. (A.C.Hartless)

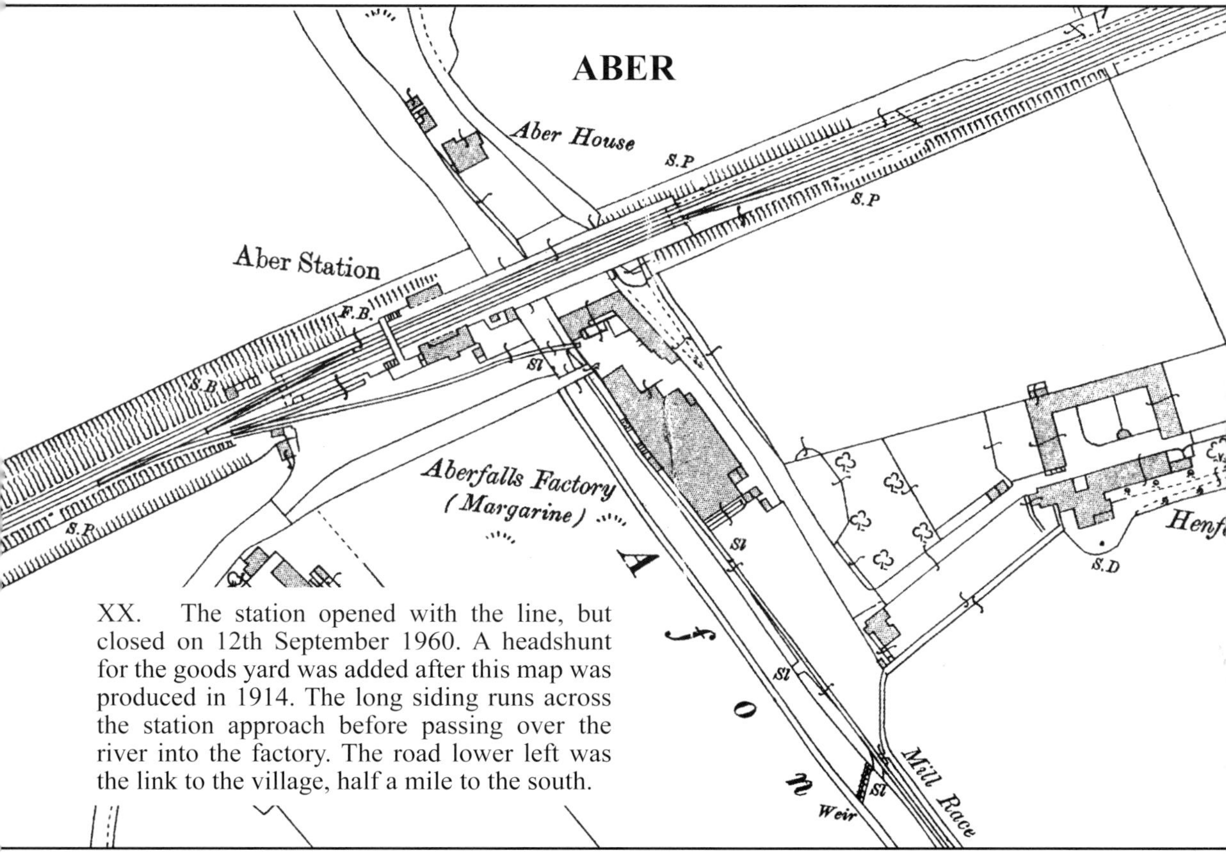

XX. The station opened with the line, but closed on 12th September 1960. A headshunt for the goods yard was added after this map was produced in 1914. The long siding runs across the station approach before passing over the river into the factory. The road lower left was the link to the village, half a mile to the south.

96. This view east is from 28th August 1954 and shows that the platforms were never raised. The footbridge was added in 1894. On the right is a camping coach. (R.M.Casserley)

97. Looking in the other direction on 14th June 1963, we see the loading gauge of the goods yard, which remained open until 4th May 1964. The bridge in the foreground is over the river; the one over the lane is behind the camera. The signal box had 15 levers and closed on 13th May 1989. (D.K.Jones coll.)

EAST OF BANGOR

98. As mentioned in caption 40, the first water troughs on the route had supply problems and Aber troughs were the solution, although closer to Holyhead than ideal. The level stretch in this area had eight level crossings listed in 2005. (R.S.Carpenter coll.)

This design for a water scoop appeared in the *Proceedings of the Institution of Mechanical Engineers* in 1861. The hinge is near the floor of the water tank and the operating handle is top left. The diagram shows only the front and rear of the tender.

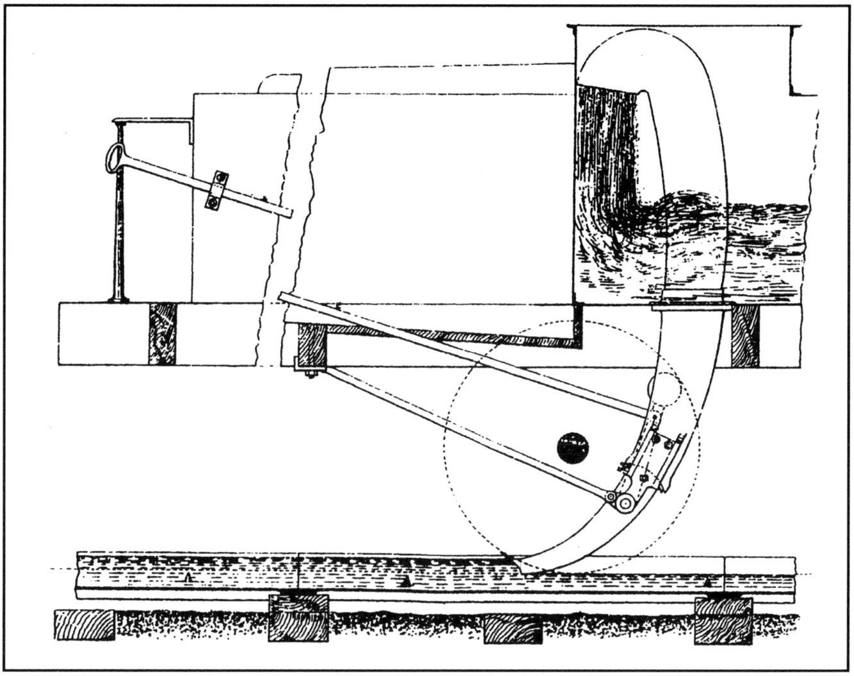

99. On the approach to Llandegi Tunnel (505yds) is Llandegi Viaduct, which is formed of 22 brick arches, with stone facings. This motor train is emerging from the west end of the tunnel, sometime in the 1930s, and is about to cross the shorter Cegin Viaduct and then to pass Penrhyn Sidings Box (12 levers, closed 28th August 1954). Next was Bethesda Junction. Its signal box had 25 levers and was closed on 1st August 1965. It also controlled two tip sidings. The line then enters Bangor Tunnel. (R.S.Carpenter coll.)

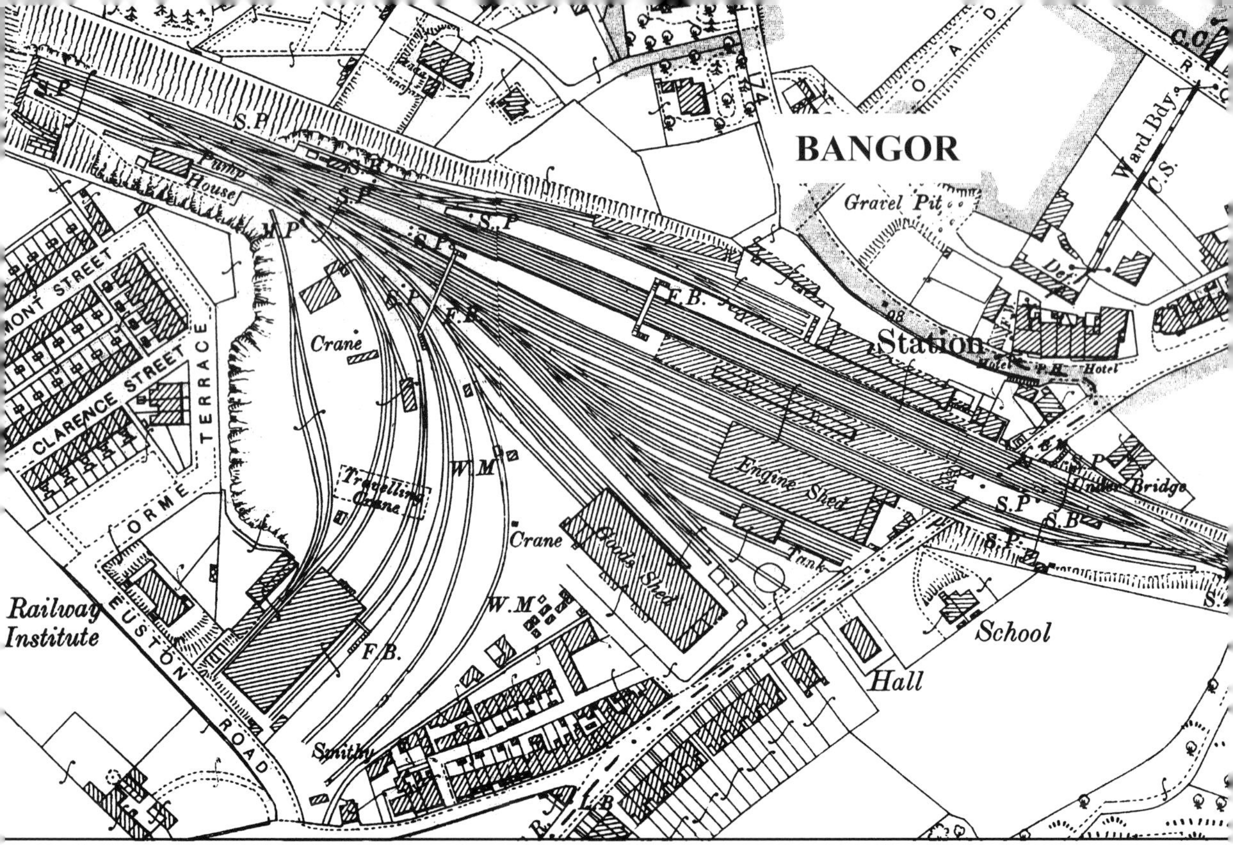

XXI. The 1900 edition is at 20ins to 1 mile and shows two footbridges away from the canopy, the left one being for staff only. On the left are the workshops, complete with a crane spanning four tracks. Belmont Tunnel is on the left and takes the line to Holyhead. It was originally 726yds in length, but was reduced to 615yds in 1881, to improve the shunting arrangements.

100. Coaches in LNWR livery stand at the up main platform, while 4-6-0 no. 1440 *Wellington* passes on the down through line in July 1924. In the background is Bangor Tunnel, which is 890yds in length. (Bentley coll.)

101. The original building is centre and the narrow yard in front of it is evident here and on the map. Major changes were starting when this photograph was taken in about 1922. Two tracks would be laid to the right of the spacious structure and it would stand on an island subsequently. The footbridge is obscured by smoke. No. 1 Box is in the foreground and would soon be demolished. (A.Dudman coll.)

102. The ticket hall was in an entirely new entrance building, seen in 1926. The doorway leads into it and from it rises a wide stairway up to the roofed footbridge seen in most of the following photographs. The entrance is still in use, but the gateway has long gone. (A.Dudman coll.)

103. Platforms 3 and 4, plus part of the locomotive depot, were recorded on 2nd August 1952. The shed was coded 6H, had a staff of 52 and an allocation of 29 engines at that time. (R.F.Roberts/SLS coll.)

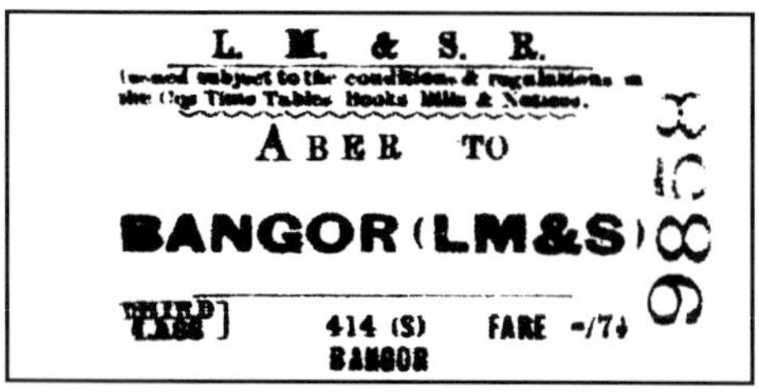

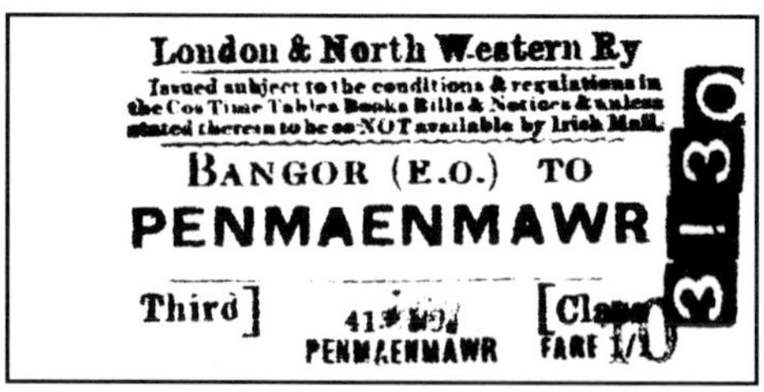

104. This closer view of the shed is from 12th August 1953 and includes nos 58903, 46604 and 52269. The compartment stock is standing at the down island platform. (H.C.Casserley)

105. An ex-LNWR Officers saloon stands in the dock road in September 1958. The building beyond it is the one seen in picture 102 and the footbridge on the right is over the two tracks mentioned in caption 101. (D.K.Jones coll.)

106. A panorama from 6th August 1961 has the short bridge seen on the left of the previous picture on the extreme left. Above it is the roof of the original station. The tracks curving on the right form part of the goods yard and in the left distance is No. 1 Box. Its 82-lever frame was in use until 8th December 1968. (E.Wilmshurst)

Other illustrations of this station can be found in *Bangor to Holyhead* and *Bangor to Portmadoc.*

➔ 107. The two extra north side tracks from the 1920s were lifted and their site was used for car parking, as seen on 16th April 1985. A class 47 is departing with the 13.20 Crewe to Holyhead. Lower left is No. 2 Box, which had a 90-lever frame, which was replaced by a panel. The platform face on the right was not used by passengers after about 1975, but tracks remained for use by the engineers. The up passenger loop (Platform 1) was split into two bays in December 1968, during rationalisation of the layout and closure of No. 1 Signal Box. At the west end, a bay was formed to accommodate the Caernarvon service which ran until January 1970. This bay was removed soon after. The eastern bay remained in use until early 1985, when the area was used to extend the station car park. (P.D.Shannon)

PLAZA
Bangor

← 108. On 24th July 1990, no. 71000 *Duke of Gloucester* was working a Holyhead to Crewe special called "The North Wales Coast Express". The two eras of buildings are clear from a fresh angle. The 4-6-2 was a prototype and in a class of its own. (T.Heavyside)

109. On 4th October 2007, no. 67014 arrived with empty stock. The coaches are in Arriva livery and such formations could often be seen on Cardiff-Holyhead services. The engine shed is still evident and contained steel. Some of the land on the right became a car park in 2011 and direct access to the down platform was provided. (R.Neville-Carlé)

Port Penrhyn Branch

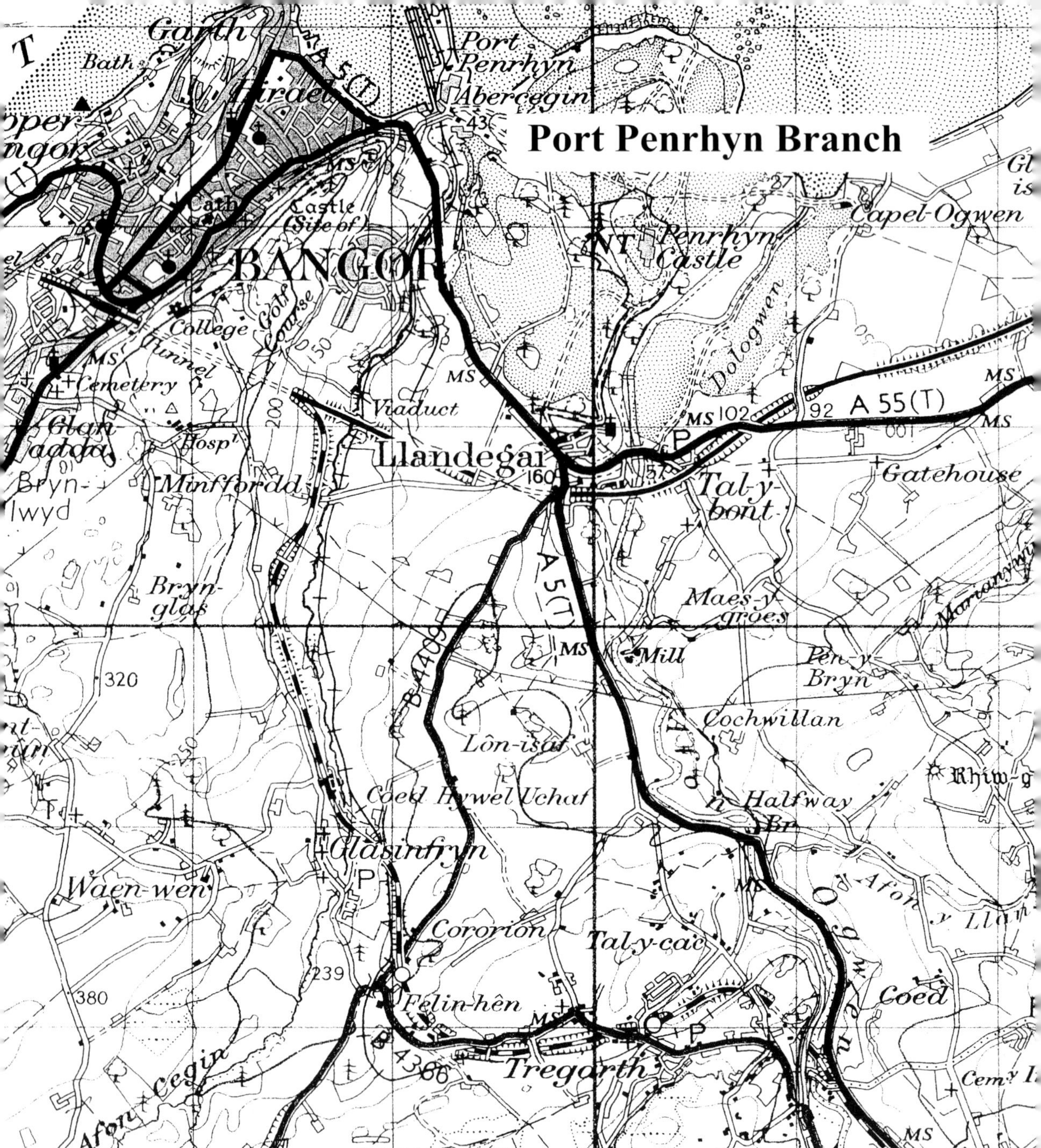

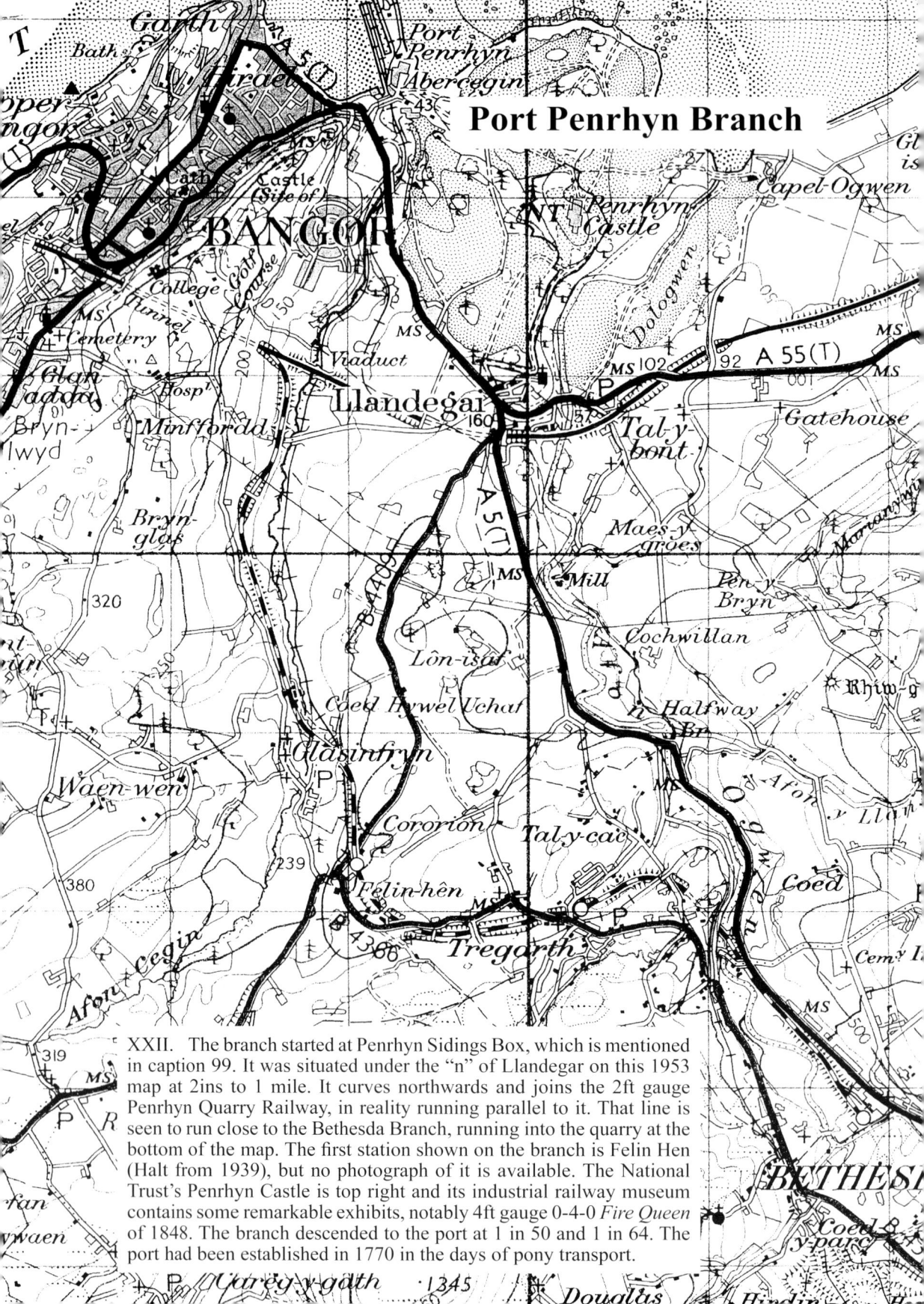

XXII. The branch started at Penrhyn Sidings Box, which is mentioned in caption 99. It was situated under the "n" of Llandegar on this 1953 map at 2ins to 1 mile. It curves northwards and joins the 2ft gauge Penrhyn Quarry Railway, in reality running parallel to it. That line is seen to run close to the Bethesda Branch, running into the quarry at the bottom of the map. The first station shown on the branch is Felin Hen (Halt from 1939), but no photograph of it is available. The National Trust's Penrhyn Castle is top right and its industrial railway museum contains some remarkable exhibits, notably 4ft gauge 0-4-0 *Fire Queen* of 1848. The branch descended to the port at 1 in 50 and 1 in 64. The port had been established in 1770 in the days of pony transport.

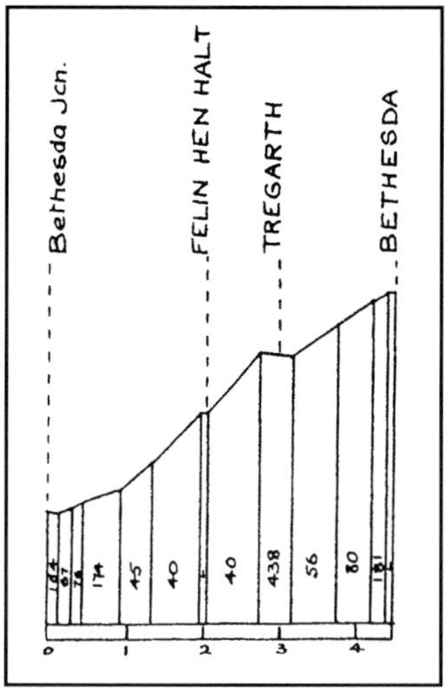

PORT PENRHYN

110. Standard gauge wagons are centre stage on 11th August 1953, while narrow gauge shunting is undertaken by *Glyder*, on the right. This was an 0-4-0WT built by Andrew Barclay in 1931 for the Durham Water Board. (H.C.Casserley)

(lower) 111. A northward view on 25th June 1956 features some novel trackwork. The first railway was opened with horse haulage in 1801. It was almost completely relaid for steam traction by 1877. (H.C.Casserley)

112. BR 2-6-2T no. 41200 is on the right on 27th June 1956, as 0-4-0ST *Blanche* leaves with a train loaded with slates. This engine was built by Hunslet in 1893 and was acquired by the Festiniog Railway in 1963, along with its sister, *Linda*. Both still work on it and were soon converted to 2-4-0TTs having been fitted with tenders; also sanders to eliminate the buckets. Note the unusual moveable crossing, where the 2ft gauge track pivotted over the standard gauge one. (A.Neale coll.)

113. The headquarters building and part of the quay were photographed on 6th August 1961. The last narrow gauge train to carry slates ran on 28th June 1964. The PQR route is now a public path. (E.Wilmshurst)

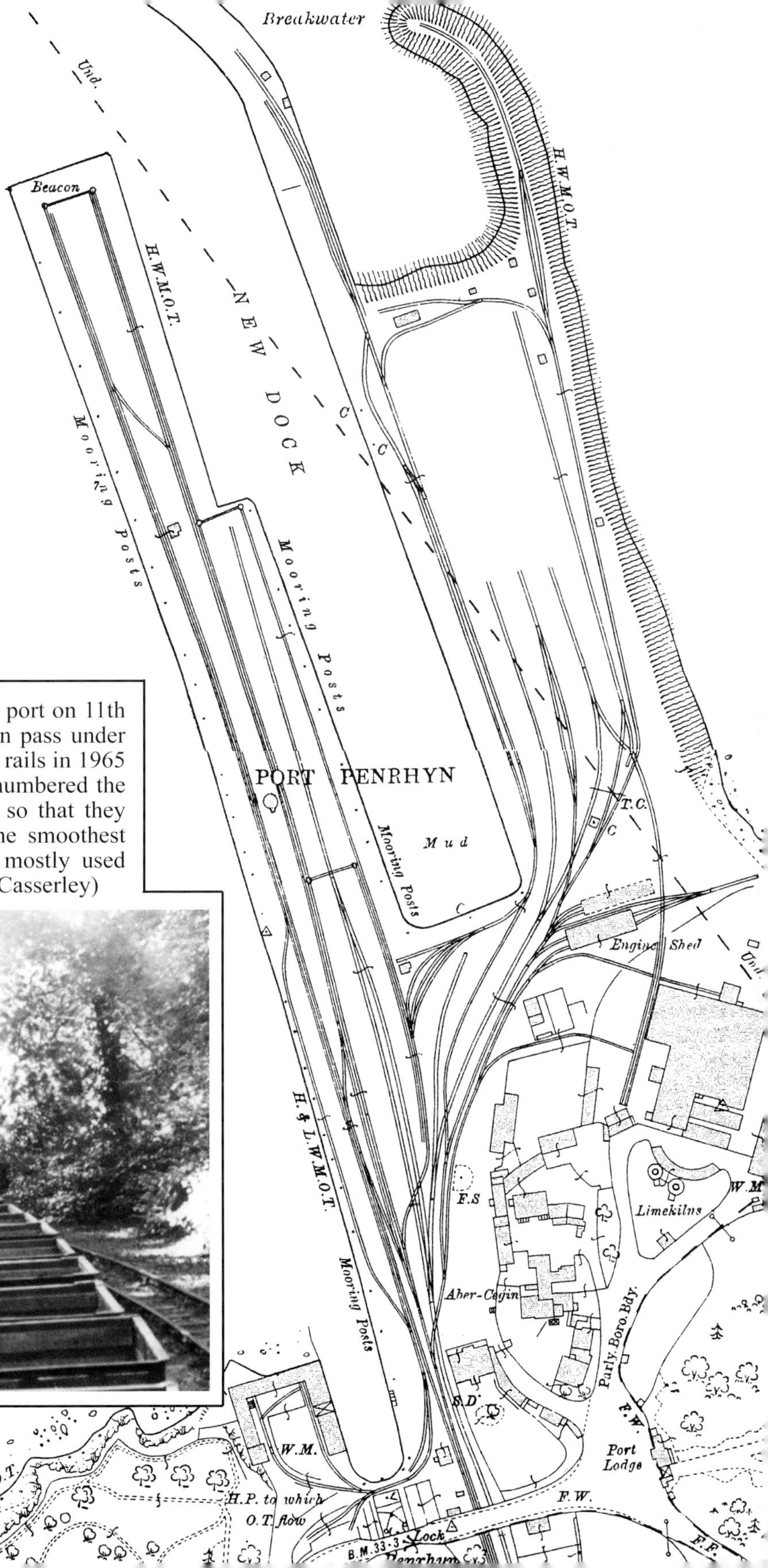

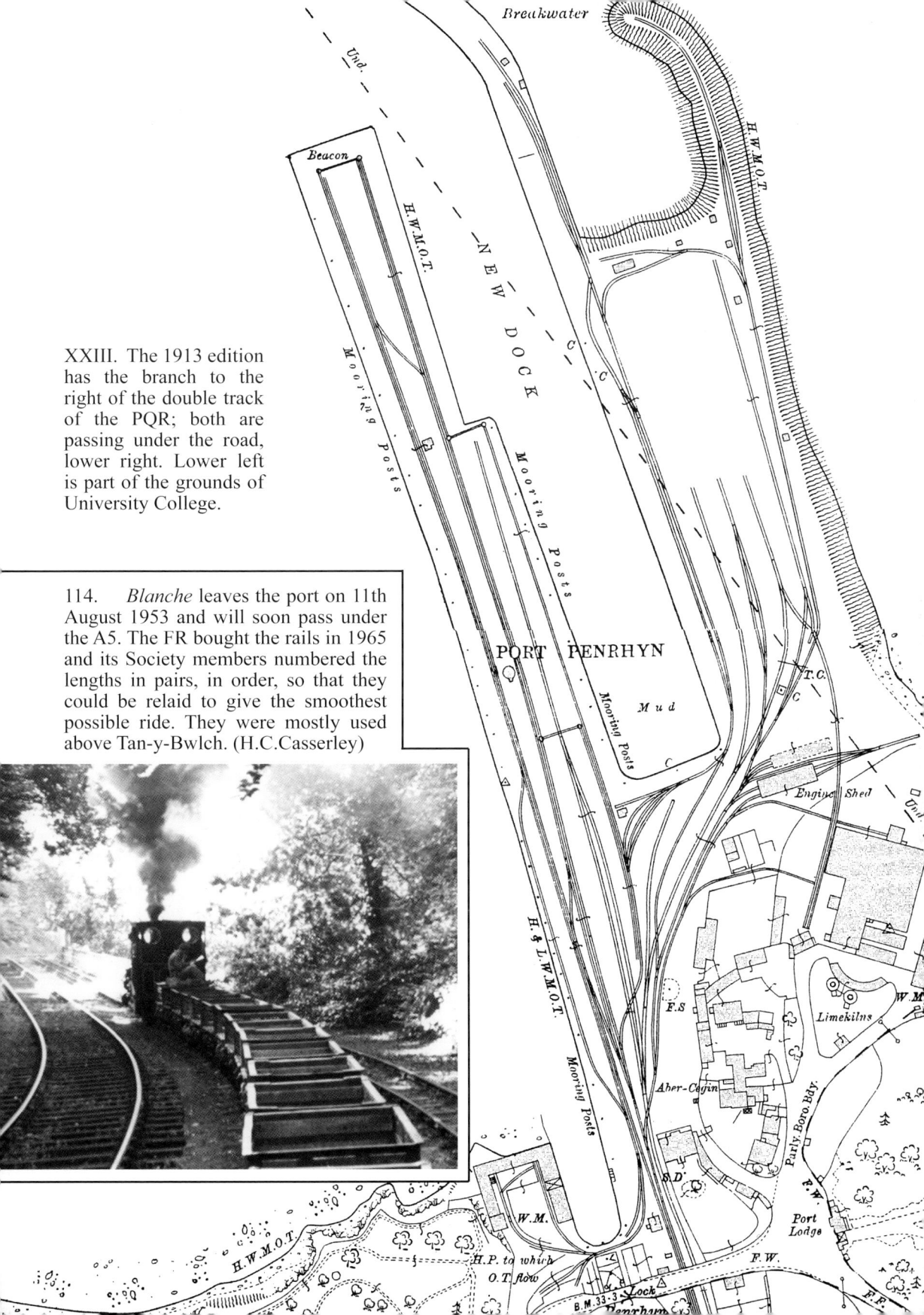

XXIII. The 1913 edition has the branch to the right of the double track of the PQR; both are passing under the road, lower right. Lower left is part of the grounds of University College.

114. *Blanche* leaves the port on 11th August 1953 and will soon pass under the A5. The FR bought the rails in 1965 and its Society members numbered the lengths in pairs, in order, so that they could be relaid to give the smoothest possible ride. They were mostly used above Tan-y-Bwlch. (H.C.Casserley)

Bethesda Branch

TREGARTH

XXIV. Our route is the upper one on this 1914 extract, the PQR being the lower one.

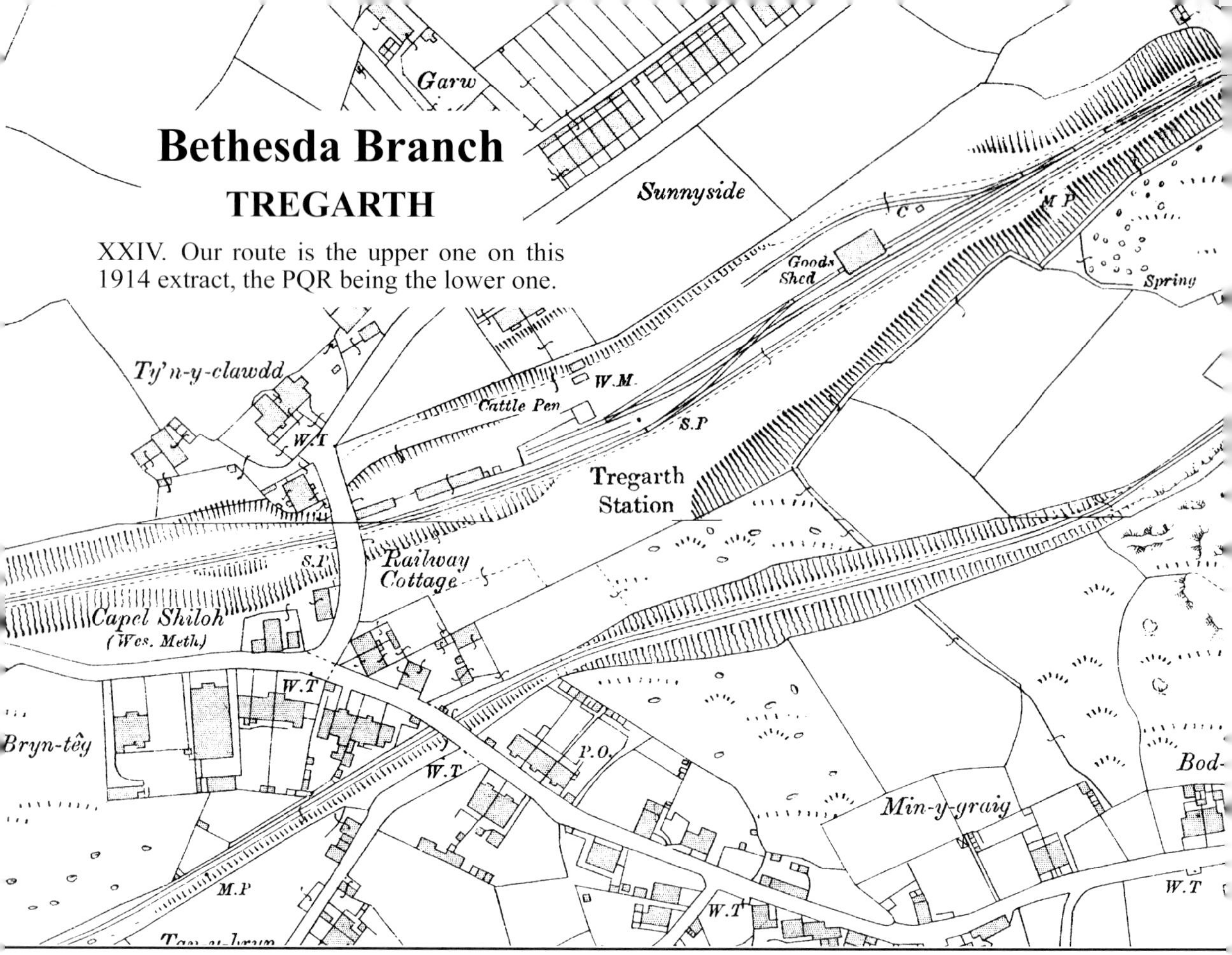

↙ 115. The road bridge is in the background as the porter waits for locals to board the train for Bethesda, probably in the 1930s. There were as many as 16 trains each way in that decade. The locomotive is an ex-LNWR 0-6-2T. (Lens of Sutton coll.)

116. Being devoid of seats, this picture may be post-closure in 1951. The road continued to the goods yard, which handled only coal after that time. (M.Whitehouse coll.)

BETHESDA

XXV. The 1914 survey reveals that there was no link with the PQR here, as most slate transfer work was done at Port Penrhyn. The population was 5281 in 1901 and so the demand for domestic coal and goods would have been good. The gasworks can be seen to have its own platform. A strike in 1900-03 reduced the number of residents and it was down to 4180 in 1961. The town had 27 chapels at its peak, plus its own hospital. This was once busy when there were over 3000 quarrymen working here.

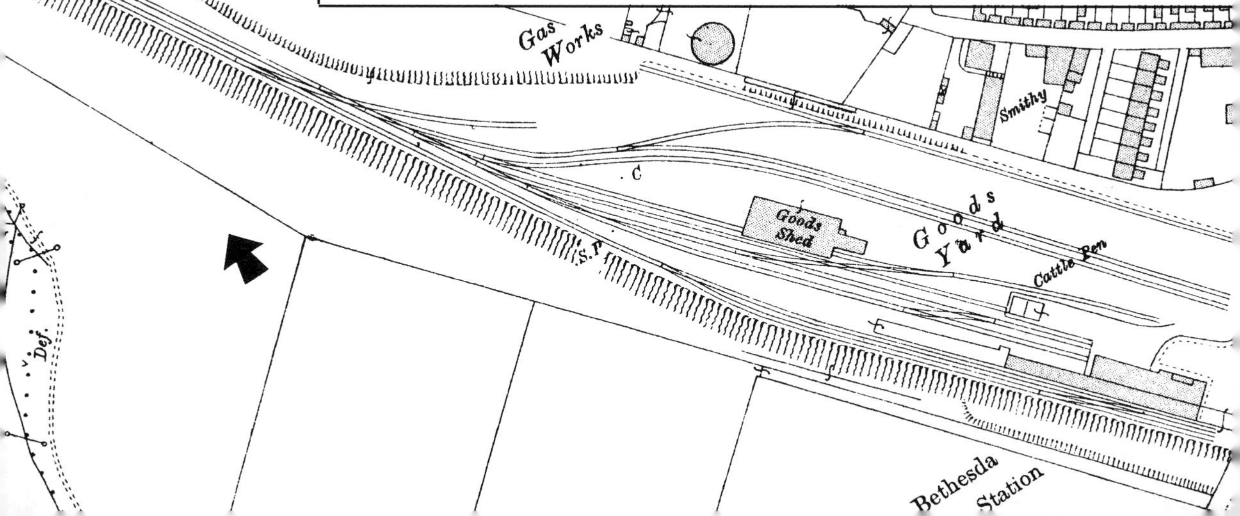

117. Attached to a horsebox in June 1947 is 0-6-2T no. 27603. Railmotors were tried on the branch in 1906-09, but they were often short of steam. These lines and the platform were removed five years after passenger service ceased in 1951. (M.Whitehouse coll.)

118. The 8.24am from Bangor has arrived behind ex-LNWR 0-6-2T no. 58903 on 7th October 1949. One engine in steam operation came to the branch in February 1954 and the 10-lever frame on the station was removed. (P.Q.Treloar coll.)

119. The impressive exterior was photographed on 19th July 1963. Many LNWR design features had been incorporated. The altitude is just over 400ft above sea level. (R.M.Casserley)

120. The goods yard closed on 7th October 1963; its crane was rated at 5-ton capacity. The last train ran on 20th October 1963 and was hauled by class 2P 2-6-2T no. 41234. The SLS tour started at Manchester Exchange and included the branches to Llanberis and Nantlle, all for 39 shillings. Happy days! (W.A.Camwell/SLS)

A
Abergavenny to Merthyr C 91 8
Abertillery and Ebbw Vale Lines D 84 5
Aberystwyth to Carmarthen E 90 1
Allhallows - Branch Line to A 62 8
Alton - Branch Lines to A 11 6
Andover to Southampton A 82 6
Ascot - Branch Lines around A 64 2
Ashburton - Branch Line to B 95 4
Ashford - Steam to Eurostar B 67 1
Ashford to Dover A 48 2
Austrian Narrow Gauge D 04 3
Avonmouth - BL around D 42 5
Aylesbury to Rugby D 91 3

B
Baker Street to Uxbridge D 90 6
Bala to Llandudno E 87 1
Banbury to Birmingham D 27 2
Banbury to Cheltenham E 63 5
Bangor to Holyhead F 01 7
Bangor to Portmadoc E 72 7
Barking to Southend C 80 2
Barmouth to Pwllheli E 53 6
Barry - Branch Lines around D 50 0
Bath Green Park to Bristol C 36 9
Bath to Evercreech Junction A 60 4
Beamish 40 years on rails E94 9
Bedford to Wellingborough D 31 9
Birmingham to Wolverhampton E253
Bletchley to Cambridge D 94 4
Bletchley to Rugby E 07 9
Bodmin - Branch Lines around B 83 1
Bournemouth to Evercreech Jn A 46 8
Bournemouth to Weymouth A 57 4
Bradshaws Guide 1866 F 05 5
Bradshaws Rail Times 1850 F 13 0
Bradshaws Rail Times 1895 F 11 6
Branch Lines series - see town names
Brecon to Neath D 43 2
Brecon to Newport D 16 6
Brecon to Newtown E 06 2
Brighton to Eastbourne A 16 1
Brighton to Worthing A 03 1
Bromley South to Rochester B 23 7
Bromsgrove to Birmingham D 87 6
Bromsgrove to Gloucester D 73 9
Brunel - A railtour D 74 6
Bude - Branch Line to B 29 9
Burnham to Evercreech Jn B 68 0

C
Cambridge to Ely D 55 5
Canterbury - BLs around B 58 9
Cardiff to Dowlais (Cae Harris) E 47 5
Cardiff to Pontypridd E 95 6
Cardiff to Swansea E 42 0
Carlisle to Hawick E 85 7
Carmarthen to Fishguard E 66 6
Caterham & Tattenham Corner B251
Central & Southern Spain NG E 91 8
Chard and Yeovil - BLs a C 30 7
Charing Cross to Dartford A 75 8
Charing Cross to Orpington A 96 3
Cheddar - Branch Line to B 90 9
Cheltenham to Andover C 43 7
Cheltenham to Redditch D 81 4
Chester to Rhyl E 93 2
Chichester to Portsmouth A 14 7
Clacton and Walton - BLs to F 04 8
Clapham Jn to Beckenham Jn B 36 7
Cleobury Mortimer - BLs a E 18 5
Clevedon & Portishead - BLs to D180
Colonel Stephens - His Empire D 62 3
Consett to South Shields E 57 4
Cornwall Narrow Gauge D 56 2
Corris and Vale of Rheidol E 65 9
Craven Arms to Llandeilo E 35 2
Craven Arms to Wellington E 33 8
Crawley to Littlehampton A 34 5
Cromer - Branch Lines around C 26 0
Croydon to East Grinstead B 48 0
Crystal Palace & Catford Loop B 87 1
Cyprus Narrow Gauge E 13 0

D
Darjeeling Revisited F 09 3
Darlington Leamside Newcastle E 28 4
Darlington to Newcastle D 98 2
Dartford to Sittingbourne B 34 3
Derwent Valley - BL to the D 06 7
Devon Narrow Gauge E 09 3
Didcot to Banbury D 02 9
Didcot to Swindon C 84 0
Didcot to Winchester C 13 0
Dorset & Somerset NG D 76 0
Douglas - Laxey - Ramsey E 75 8
Douglas to Peel C 88 8
Douglas to Port Erin C 55 0
Douglas to Ramsey D 39 5
Dover to Ramsgate A 78 9
Dublin Northwards in 1950s E 31 4
Dunstable - Branch Lines to E 27 7

E
Ealing to Slough C 42 0
East Cornwall Mineral Railways D 22 7
East Croydon to Three Bridges A 53 6
Eastern Spain Narrow Gauge E 56 7
East Grinstead - BLs to A 07 9
East London - Branch Lines of C 44 4
East London Line B 80 0
East of Norwich - Branch Lines E 69 7
Effingham Junction - BLs a A 74 1
Ely to Norwich C 90 1
Enfield Town & Palace Gates D 32 6
Epsom to Horsham A 30 7
Eritrean Narrow Gauge E 38 3
Euston to Harrow & Wealdstone C 89 5
Exeter to Barnstaple B 15 2
Exeter to Newton Abbot C 49 9
Exeter to Tavistock B 69 5
Exmouth - Branch Lines to B 00 8

F
Fairford - Branch Line to A 52 9
Falmouth, Helston & St. Ives C 74 1
Fareham to Salisbury A 67 3
Faversham to Dover B 05 3
Felixstowe & Aldeburgh - BL to D 20 3
Fenchurch Street to Barking C 20 8
Festiniog - 50 yrs of enterprise C 83 3
Festiniog 1946-55 E 01 7
Festiniog in the Fifties B 68 8
Festiniog in the Sixties B 91 6
Finsbury Park to Alexandra Pal C 02 8
Frome to Bristol B 77 0

G
Gloucester to Bristol D 35 7
Gloucester to Cardiff D 66 1
Gosport - Branch Lines around A 36 9
Greece Narrow Gauge D 72 2

H
Hampshire Narrow Gauge D 36 4
Harrow to Watford D 14 2
Harwich & Hadleigh - BLs to F 02 4
Hastings to Ashford A 37 6
Hawkhurst - Branch Line to A 66 6
Hayling - Branch Line to A 12 3
Hay-on-Wye - BL around D 92 0
Haywards Heath to Seaford A 28 4
Hemel Hempstead - BLs to D 88 3
Henley, Windsor & Marlow C77 2
Hereford to Newport D 54 8
Hertford & Hatfield - BLs a E 58 1
Hertford Loop E 71 0
Hexham to Carlisle D 75 3
Hexham to Hawick F 08 6
Hitchin to Peterborough D 07 4
Holborn Viaduct to Lewisham A 81 9
Horsham - Branch Lines to A 02 4
Huntingdon - Branch Line to A 93 2

I
Ilford to Shenfield C 97 0
Ilfracombe - Branch Line to B 21 3
Industrial Rlys of the South East A 09 3
Ipswich to Saxmundham C 41 3
Isle of Wight Lines - 50 yrs C 12 3

K
Kent Narrow Gauge C 45 1
Kidderminster to Shrewsbury E 10 9
Kingsbridge - Branch Line to C 98 7
Kings Cross to Potters Bar E 62 8
Kingston & Hounslow Loops A 83 3
Kingswear - Branch Line to C 17 8

L
Lambourn - Branch Line to C 70 3
Launceston & Princetown C 19 2
Lewisham to Dartford A 92 5
Lines around Wimbledon B 75 6
Liverpool Street to Chingford D 01 2
Liverpool Street to Ilford C 34 5
Llandeilo to Swansea E 46 8
London Bridge to Addiscombe B 20 6
London Bridge to East Croydon A 58 1
Longmoor - Branch Lines to A 41 3
Looe - Branch Line to C 22 2
Lowestoft - BLs around E 40 6
Ludlow to Hereford E 14 7
Lydney - Branch Lines around E 26 0
Lyme Regis - Branch Line to A 45 1
Lynton - Branch Line to B 04 6

M
Machynlleth to Barmouth E 54 3
Maesteg and Tondu Lines E 06 2
March - Branch Lines around B 09 1
Marylebone to Rickmansworth D 49 4
Melton Constable to Yarmouth Bch E031
Midhurst - Branch Lines of E 78 9
Mitcham Junction Lines B 01 5
Mitchell & company C 59 8
Monmouth - Branch Lines to E 20 8
Monmouthshire Eastern Valleys D 71 5
Moretonhampstead - BL to C 27 7
Moreton-in-Marsh to Worcester D 26 5
Mountain Ash to Neath D 80 7

N
Newbury to Westbury C 66 6
Newcastle to Hexham D 69 2
Newport (IOW) - Branch Lines to A 26 0
Newquay - Branch Lines to C 71 0
Newton Abbot to Plymouth C 60 4
Newtown to Aberystwyth E 41 3
North East German NG D 44 9
Northern France Narrow Gauge C 75 8
Northern Spain Narrow Gauge E 83 3
North London Line B 94 7
North Woolwich - BLs around C 65 9

O
Ongar - Branch Line to E 05 5
Oswestry - Branch Lines around E 60 4
Oswestry to Whitchurch E 81 9
Oxford to Bletchley D 57 9
Oxford to Moreton-in-Marsh D 15 9

P
Paddington to Ealing C 37 6
Paddington to Princes Risborough C819
Padstow - Branch Line to B 54 1
Peterborough to Kings Lynn E 32 1
Plymouth - BLs around B 98 5
Plymouth to St. Austell C 63 5
Pontypool to Mountain Ash D 65 4
Pontypridd to Merthyr F 14 7
Pontypridd to Port Talbot E 86 4
Porthmadog 1954-94 - BL a B 31 2
Portmadoc 1923-46 - BLa a B 13 8
Portsmouth to Southampton A 31 4
Portugal Narrow Gauge E 67 3
Potters Bar to Cambridge D 70 8
Princes Risborough - BL to D 05 0
Princes Risborough to Banbury C 85 7

R
Reading to Basingstoke B 27 5
Reading to Didcot C 79 6
Reading to Guildford A 47 5
Redhill to Ashford A 73 4
Return to Blaenau 1970-82 C 64 2
Rhyl to Bangor F 15 4
Rhymney & New Tredegar Lines E 48 2
Rickmansworth to Aylesbury D 61 6
Romania & Bulgaria NG E 23 9
Romneyrail C 32 1
Ross-on-Wye - BLs around E 30 7
Ruabon to Barmouth E 84 0
Rugby to Birmingham E 37 6
Rugby to Loughborough F 12 3
Rugby to Stafford F 07 9
Ryde to Ventnor A 19 2

S
Salisbury to Westbury B 39 8
Saxmundham to Yarmouth C 69 7
Saxony Narrow Gauge D 47 0
Seaton & Sidmouth - BLs to A 95 6
Selsey - Branch Line to A 04 8
Sheerness - Branch Line to B 16 2
Shenfield to Ipswich E 96 3
Shrewsbury - Branch Line to A 86 4
Shrewsbury to Chester E 70 3
Shrewsbury to Ludlow E 21 5
Shrewsbury to Newtown E 29 1
Sierra Leone Narrow Gauge D 28 9
Sirhowy Valley Line E 12 3
Sittingbourne to Ramsgate A 90 1
Slough to Newbury C 56 7
South African Two-foot gauge E 51 2
Southampton to Bournemouth A 42 0
Southend & Southminster BLs E 76 5
Southern France Narrow Gauge C 47 5
South London Line B 46 6
South Lynn to Norwich City F 03 1
Southwold - Branch Line to A 15 4
Spalding - Branch Lines around E 52 9
St Albans to Bedford D 08 1
St. Austell to Penzance C 67 3
Steaming through West Hants A 69 7
Stourbridge to Wolverhampton E 16 1
St. Pancras to Barking D 68 5
St. Pancras to Folkestone E 88 8
St. Pancras to St. Albans C 78 9
Stratford-u-Avon to Birmingham
Stratford-u-Avon to Cheltenham C
ST the Isle of Wight A 56 7
Surrey Narrow Gauge C 87 1
Sussex Narrow Gauge C 68 0
Swanley to Ashford B 45 9
Swansea to Carmarthen E 59 8
Swindon to Bristol C 96 3
Swindon to Gloucester D 46 3
Swindon to Newport D 30 2
Swiss Narrow Gauge C 94 9

T
Talyllyn 60 E 98 7
Taunton to Barnstaple B 60 2
Taunton to Exeter C 82 6
Tavistock to Plymouth B 88 6
Tenterden - Branch Line to A 21 5
Three Bridges to Brighton A 35 2
Tilbury Loop C 86 4
Tiverton - BLS a C 62 8
Tivetshall to Beccles D 41 8
Tonbridge to Hastings A 44 4
Torrington - Branch Lines to B 37
Towcester - BLs around E 39 0
Tunbridge Wells BLs A 32 1

U
Upwell - Branch Line to B 64 0

V
Victoria to Bromley South A 98 7
Vivarais Revisited E 08 6

W
Wantage - Branch Line to D 25 8
Wareham to Swanage 50 yrs D0
Waterloo to Windsor A 54 3
Waterloo to Woking A 38 3
Watford to Leighton Buzzard D 45
Welshpool to Llanfair E 49 9
Wenford Bridge to Fowey C 09 3
Westbury to Bath B 55 8
Westbury to Taunton C 76 5
West Cornwall Mineral Rlys D 48
West Croydon to Epsom B 08 4
West German Narrow Gauge D 9
West London - BLs of C 50 5
West London Line B 84 8
West Wiltshire - BLs of D 12 8
Weymouth - BLs A 65 9
Willesden Jn to Richmond B 71 8
Wimbledon to Beckenham C 58 1
Wimbledon to Epsom B 62 6
Wimborne - BLs around A 97 0
Wisbech - BLs a C 01 7
Witham & Kelvedon - BLs a E 82
Woking to Alton A 59 8
Woking to Portsmouth A 25 3
Woking to Southampton A 55 0
Wolverhampton to Shrewsbury E
Worcester to Birmingham D 97 5
Worcester to Hereford D 38 8
Worthing to Chichester A 06 2

Y
Yeovil - 50 yrs change C 38 3
Yeovil to Dorchester A 76 5
Yeovil to Exeter A 91 8